The Good Deal Directory Factory Shopping & Sightseeing Guide to the U.K.

Sponsored By Clarks Factory
Shopping Village

The Good Deal Directory Company
also publishes
The Good Deal Directory 1996.

This 608-page book contains more than 2,300 outlets where
you can buy brand name goods at bargain prices.
It costs just £9.99 (free p&p) from
PO Box 4, Lechlade, Glos GL7 3YB
(cheques made payable to The Good Deal Directory).
Or you can phone the credit card hotline on
01367 860016.

.

Why you can't afford to be without The Good Deal Directory 1996

.

You can find out how to dress like a queen on
a scullery maid's wages!

.

Have a home that's smart enough to appear in Homes & Gardens
magazine without a Country Life income

.

No other book covers as many areas of the world of
discount retailing

.

Brand names found at bargain prices in
The Good Deal Directory 1996 include:
Aquascutum, Barbour, Burberry, Cerrruti 1881, Charnos lingerie,
Descamps, Dunhill, Edinburgh Crystal, Jaeger, Joan & David shoes,
Levi's, Mamas & Papas, Minton bone china, Mulberry, Next, Nicole
Farhi, Oash Kosh b'Gosh, Paul Costelloe, Polo Ralph Lauren, Racing
Green, Spode, Timberland, Villeroy & Boch, Wedgwood, Windsmoor
and Wrangler.

The Good Deal Directory covers the areas of women's and men's
clothes, children's clothes and nursery equipment, household and
giftware, electrical equipment, diy and renovation, furniture and soft
furnishings, food and leisure.

First published in 1996 by

The Good Deal Directory Company Limited P.O. Box 4, Lechlade, Glos GL7 3YB

ISBN 0-9526529-5-1

Typeset by Windmill Typesetters, 87-89 Saffron Hill, London EC1N 8QU.

Printed by Biddles Ltd, Woodbridge Park Estate, Woodbridge Road, Guildford, Surrey GU1 1DA.

The Good Deal Directory
Factory Shopping
& Sightseeing Guide
to the U.K.

NOELLE WALSH

CONTENTS

INTRODUCTION

A s the millions of visitors to Britain's shores each year can testify, there are still many things about this island that even the British, with their natural aversion to self-promotion, can feel justly proud. Prominent among these is the visual richness and incredible variety of its countryside. Where else in the world in an area of only 94,000 square miles can be found such a diversity of terrain from low-lying wetlands to rolling hills and magisterial mountains? And within this diverse environment, as its communities developed from the coming of the Beaker folk to the present day, there has grown such a rich profusion of architecture that in many areas of the country a simple day's touring can bear witness to the passing of 5000 years as you encounter buildings from the Stone Age to the present day.

This book has been designed to help you enjoy some fragments of this cultural and historical legacy whilst at the same time visiting some of the outlets that offer the very best of British manufacture at discounted prices. The idea is that while enjoying a holiday or even a day out you can combine sightseeing with shopping, a pleasure that I have indulged in for many years. It might seem, on the surface, to be adding to the cost of your holiday or day out. However, when you consider what you might otherwise have spent on the same goods in your local retail outlet, you will soon get to enjoy it!

You can dip in and out of these suggested tours and make them as long or short as you want. Depending on how long you spend at each site they can take a day or longer. Some of the great houses and palaces that I have included have several aspects to a tour. In some cases you can pay to visit the house and grounds or just the house alone and vice versa and there may also be other tours available connected with the site. How long you spend there will be dictated by your pocket and degree of interest – probably both!

Apart from the central London tours, it wouldn't really be practical to attempt them without a car. Most of the sites to visit are out in the great British countryside where bus and train time tables would make dropping in at two or three in a day fairly impractical.

We've included maps at the beginning of each section to give the general position and geographical relationship of each site but a road atlas would still be essential. As far as specific directions in each town are concerned these generally haven't been given as to do so would have virtually doubled the length and price of the book! Most of the discount outlets are in small towns and villages where they are well known to the locals and I have found that just stopping and asking always does the trick. Telephone numbers for each tourist site and factory shop have always been given in the Factfile at the end of each tour so, if you're worried, just phone and get local directions before you set off. Most of the tourist sites are well sign posted when you arrive in their vicinity.

Always check the opening hours of each shop and days of opening in the Factfile. Some of the factory shops are not open on Sundays and one or two are only open at certain times of the year. A problem with any business, too, is that they can close down or move – so always phone to check that they're still operating and from that site. The same, of course, goes for the tourist sites where opening times generally vary between winter and summer months, Easter normally being the point where they get into full swing. There are some wonderful sites in Britain (often Museums and Art collections) where there is no admission fee but at most sites there is a charge and rates vary for adults, children, OAPs and (in some cases) for the unemployed. If you're going with the family bear in mind that most tourist sites offer a special 'family' price. There is also usually a last time of admission so, although the site may be open until later, you cannot be admitted as you would have too little time to go round.

All the factory shops and discount outlets detailed in this book are open to the general public and there is no charge to go into them although if you're wanting to do a tour of the factory itself there may well be a charge for this. Again look at the Factfile and it will tell you. Most enjoyable holidays or day trips will repay a little careful planning so before you set off always check the Factfile first to make sure that the site or outlet is actually open on the day you want to visit, plan your route and if you're not sure of anything phone first!

LONDON AND THE SOUTHERN COUNTIES

This is a rather arbitrary grouping covering an area possessing a widely disparate variety of sites and scenery. Suffice it to say that London, as well as possessing some wonderful shopping opportunities, offers some of the most interesting and exciting tourism venues of any capital city in the world. It has magnificent architecture, a majestic river and abounds with sites of profound cultural and historical significance. The counties that border it are too different in character and appearance to be dealt with by any comfortable generalisation but any visitor will be delighted to find that within a short journey of the capital city are to be found tranquil and delightful villages and stately homes and gardens magnificent in their ancient grandeur.

TOUR 1
Central London – Madame Tussauds, The Royal Academy and the Wallace Collection

There are a number of interesting factory shops in Central London that are virtually next door to places of interest to the tourist or sightseer. Whether you could combine visits to all of these outlets and sites on one day rather depends on how long you want to spend shopping or sightseeing at each but it is unlikely that you would have time for all of them – after all you could probably spend several days at the British Museum without feeling you had taken in everything!

You might want to start your Central London tour, as many visitors to the capital do, with a visit to **Madame Tussaud's** famous waxwork museum on the Marylebone Rd next to Baker St underground station. Sited here since 1884, the collection features life-like models of famous historical figures, kings, queens, politicians, sportstars and the like. There are also themed areas within the exhibition such as 'Hollywood Legends' and another popular attraction is 'The Spirit of London', a journey in a time taxi which summons up the atmosphere of London over the last 300 years through sights, sounds and smells.

From here, with bargain shopping for classic quality ladies wear in mind, a three minute walk down Luxborough St (opposite Madame Tussauds on the other side of Marylebone Rd) will bring you to Paddington St where at number 39 is situated **Discount Dressing.** This is a veritable Aladdin's cave of designer bargains. They sell mostly German, Italian and French designer labels at prices at least 50% and up to 90% below those in normal retail outlets, and all items are brand new and perfect. They have a team of buyers all over Europe who purchase stock directly from the manufacturer, therefore by-passing the importers and wholesalers and, of course, their mark-up. They also buy bankrupt stock in this country. Their agreement with their suppliers means that they are not able to advertise brand names for obvious reasons, but they are all well-known for their top quality and style. So confident is Discount Dressing that you will be unable to find the same item cheaper elsewhere, that they offer to give the outfit to you free of charge should you perform this miracle. Merchandise includes raincoats, dresses, suits, trousers, blouses, evening wear, special occasion outfits and jackets, in sizes 6-24 and in some cases larger.

A classic bargain shopping opportunity for men is situated about a mile from here in Avery Row which is about two or three minutes walk from Bond St underground station. This is the **Paul Smith Sale Shop** which offers year-round seconds and ends of lines in the heart of London's West End. This sale shop has stock from last season, so it is always a season behind, and sells at discounts of 40%-50%. There are lots of bargain bins and a wide selection of accessories from belts and cologne to cuff links. As with all permanent sale shops, stock varies, so you may or may not be lucky.

On leaving here you are only a few minutes walk down Bond Street from Burlington House which is next to the Burlington Arcade and is the home of the **Royal Academy of Arts.** The house was built in in 1664 but the Academy itself was founded in 1768 by King George lll and has since become Britain's premier fine arts institution – often being host to superb exhibitions at various times during the year.

For women's casual wear you are no distance here from the **Ton Sur Ton factory shop** at 35 Riding House St which is just off Langham Place at the northern end of Regent St. This European casual wear company which sells tracksuits, sweatshirts, T-shirts in unusual colours and soft fabrics, has a factory outlet in the heart of London's rag trade area. The company also sells denim, a fitness range, training shoes, rugby shirts, jackets, jeans and accessories. The factory outlet sells samples, returns and perfect garments at at least 50% of their normal retail price, and lower in a number of cases.

A brisk walk west of here along Wigmore St and right up Duke St will then take you to Manchester Square where the **Wallace Collection** is kept at 18th century Hertford House. This comprises one of the premier art collections in the whole of the UK and was a gift to the nation by the French wife of Richard Wallace, the son of the 4th Marquis of Hertford. The collection contains various superb representations of 18th century French art with paintings by Watteau, Boucher and Fragonard and also works by Hals, Gainsborough, Rubens, Delacroix and Titian. There is also a superb collection of furniture, porcelain, clocks and armour (the largest collection outside the Tower of London).

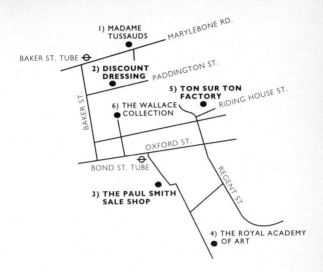

FACTFILE

1) Madame Tussauds
MARYLEBONE RD, LONDON NW1
TEL: 0171 935 6861
Open: All year 10am - 5.30 pm (9.30am weekends, 9.00am summer)
closed Christmas day. Admission: £8.75 (children under 16 £5.75,
OAPs £6.60)

2) Discount Dressing
39 PADDINGTON ST, LONDON W1M 3RN
TEL: 0171 486 7230
Open: 10am - 6pm seven days a week

3) The Paul Smith Sale Shop
23 AVERY ROW, LONDON W1
TEL: 0171 493 1287
Open: 10.30am - 6.30pm Monday - Friday, 10am - 7pm Thursday,
10am - 6pm Saturday

4) The Royal Academy of Arts

BURLINGTON HOUSE, PICCADILLY, LONDON W1
TEL: 0171 439 7438 & 0171 439 4996/7
Open: All year daily 10am - 6 pm (closed 24th, 25th, 26th December
and Good Friday) Admission: Average admission charge depending on
exhibition £5, concessions between £3.50 - £4

5) Ton Sur Ton Factory Shop

35 RIDING HOUSE STREET, LONDON W1 7PT
TEL: 0171 637 3473.
Open: 10.30am - 5pm Monday - Friday

6) The Wallace Collection

HERTFORD HOUSE, MANCHESTER SQUARE, LONDON W1M 6BN
TEL: 0171 935 0687
Open: All year Monday - Saturday 10am - 5pm,
Sunday 2pm - 5pm (closed Good Friday, May Day, 24th, 25th, 26th
December and 1st January). Admission: Free

TOUR 2
*The East End of London – Hackney,
Bethnal Green, Bow, the Tower of London
and Dickens House*

This tour takes us into the Cockney heartland of London known as the
East End. The houses are not so grand (although here and there there
are still some fine Georgian rows that escaped the Blitz) but there's still
plenty of interest and some fine bargain shopping to be done if you
know where to look.

You'll probably need a car for this tour which begins at the **Burberry
factory shop** at 29-53 Chatham Place, Hackney. As with their Welsh
outlet (page 51), this Burberry factory shop sells the full range of
Burberry merchandise, none of which is current stock. There are
seconds and overmakes of the famous name raincoats and duffle coats
as well as accessories such as the distinctive umbrellas, scarves and
handbags. All carry the Burberry label and are about one third off the
normal retail price. Childrenswear tends to be thin on the ground, but

there are plenty of gift items such as Burberry brand name teas, coffees, chocolate and marmalade. The large warehouse has clothes set out on dozens of rails and although the surroundings are relatively spartan, the outlet is often full of tourists.

Here you are a minute's drive from Mare St. Reaching Mare St, drive south in the direction of Bethnal Green. In less than a mile Mare Street becomes Cambridge Heath Rd. A couple of hundred yards down on the left is the **Bethnal Green Museum of Childhood** housed in an old Victorian Hall. The museum contains a childhood fantasy collection of dolls, doll's houses, toys, puppets, games, model theatres and model soldiers and also a children's costume and antique nursery toys collection.

Having emerged from this reverie of childhood, carrying on south down Cambridge Heath Rd will bring you to the junction with Mile End Rd. Turn left and travel east for around two miles and on the right you will see **St Mary Le Bow** church whose bells recalled Dick Whittington four times to be Lord Mayor of London and within the sound of which you must be born to be considered a true Cockney. Much of this Wren church has been restored after its destruction by German bombs and it is a fine sight that greets you if you venture indoors.

Carrying on east a short distance will bring you on the left to Fairfield Rd where are housed two exciting shopping outlets. At 75-83 Fairfield Rd is the **Nicole Farhi factory shop.** This tiny factory shop sells previous season merchandise, samples and seconds from Nicole Farhi and French Connection for women and men. Stock varies so do phone first if you have a specific requirement and particularly if you are looking for children's clothes which tend to be very seasonal. There is much more women's than menswear.

At 46-52 is **The Curtain Mill.** This permanent discount outlet has a huge choice of top quality fabrics at really low prices - from 99p a yard and includes excellent discounts on many designer labels. A large warehouse, it stocks Wilson Wilcox, Ashley Wilde, Gordon Richmond, Blendworth, among other leading names at discount prices.

Heading back west now about three miles towards the City following Bow Rd, Mile End Rd and Whitechapel brings you to Mansell St where turning left you will soon reach the **Tower of London,** perhaps the most famous castle in the world. William the Conqueror began building the castle in the 12th century but many additions and alterations were made in the 16th century by Henry VIII. Henry made almost constant use of the facilities for permanently disposing of such tiresome difficulties as his two wives, Anne Boleyn and Katherine Howard, and the martyrs Thomas More and John Fisher, and it is a bizarre fact that of the 63 bodies lying in the Tower chapel only nine still possessed their heads when interred. Such executions are now a thing of the past but you can still tour the castle and also visit the Crown Jewels exhibition.

From the Tower travel back north up Mansell St, Middlesex St and Bishopsgate to Great Eastern St which will take you to the junction with Old St. Here turn left down Old St for about three quarters of a mile which will bring you to the junction with Goswell Rd. At 101-105 Goswell Rd you will find **Stockhouse.** Formerly known as Goldsmith & Company, in late 1994 Stockhouse expanded from a purely wholesale warehouse into a trade discount centre for branded menswear that is also open to the public. It stocks more than 3,500 men's suits, from stylish business suits, formal dresswear and comfortable lounge suits to famous brand men's shirts, silk ties, blazers, sports jackets, waxed jackets, overcoats, designer swimwear, underwear, socks and branded sportswear. Sizes range from 36" chest to 54". By purchasing cancelled orders and broken ranges from famous manufacturers at clearing prices, they are able to offer famous brands at greatly reduced prices without compromising on quality or style.

About a mile from here if you take a right down Clerkenwell Rd, right again at Grays Inn Rd and a left at Roger St, is Doughty St where **Charles Dickens house** is sited at number 48. Dickens lived here for two and a half years from 1837 and it was here that he wrote the Pickwick Papers, Oliver Twist and Nicholas Nickleby. Pages from Dickens' original manuscripts are exhibited together with many other personal mementoes and the drawing room as Dickens once lived in it has been reconstructed.

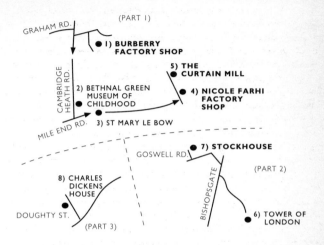

GRAHAM RD.

(PART 1)

● 1) BURBERRY
FACTORY SHOP

CAMBRIDGE HEATH RD.

2) BETHNAL GREEN
MUSEUM OF
CHILDHOOD ●

5) THE ● CURTAIN MILL

● 4) NICOLE FARHI
FACTORY
SHOP

MILE END RD.   3) ST MARY LE BOW

● 7) STOCKHOUSE

GOSWELL RD.

(PART 2)

8) CHARLES
DICKENS
HOUSE

BISHOPSGATE

DOUGHTY ST.

(PART 3)

6) TOWER OF
LONDON ●

FACTFILE

1) Burberry Factory Shop
29-53 CHATHAM PLACE, HACKNEY, LONDON E9 6LP
TEL: 0181 985 3344
Open: 12 noon - 6pm Monday - Friday, 9 am - 3pm Saturday

2) Bethnal Green Museum of Childhood
CAMBRIDGE HEATH RD, BETHNAL GREEN, LONDON E2
TEL: 0181 980 2415 OR 0181 981 1711
Open: All year, Monday - Thursday and Saturday 10am - 5.50pm,
Sunday 2.30pm - 5.50pm (closed Fri, May Day, 24th, 25th, 26th
December and 1st January). Admission: Free

3) Nicole Farhi Outlet Shop
75-83 FAIRFIELD ROAD, BOW, LONDON E3 2QR
TEL: 0181 981 3931 EXT 203
Open: 10am - 3pm Tuesday, Wednesday, Saturday, 11am - 6.30pm
Thursday, 10am - 5.30 pm Friday.

4) The Curtain Mill
46-52 FAIRFIELD ROAD, LONDON E3 2QB
TEL: 0181 980 9000
Open 9 am - 5.30pm seven days a week.

5) The Tower of London
TOWER HILL, LONDON EC3
TEL: 0171 709 0765
Open: All year, March - October , Monday - Saturday 9am - 6pm,
Sunday 10am - 6pm (last admission 5pm); November - February,
Monday - Saturday 9am - 5pm, Sunday 10am - 5pm; closed 24th,
25th, 26th December and 1st January
Admission: £8.30 (children under 16 £5.50 OAPs, Students, Disabled
& Unemployed £6.25, Family Ticket £21.95).

6) Stockhouse
101-105 GOSWELL ROAD, LONDON EC1V 7ER
TEL: 0171-253 5761
Open 9am - 5pm Monday - Friday, 9am 1.30pm Sunday,
closed Saturdays

7) Dickens House Museum
48 DOUGHTY ST, LONDON WC1N 2LF
TEL: 0171 405 2127
Open: All year, Monday - Saturday 10am - 5pm last admission
4.30pm closed Sundays, some public holidays and Christmas.
Admission £3 (children £1, OAPs & Students £2)

TOUR 3
Kings Rd, The National Army Museum,
Carlyle's House – Cheyne Row,
New King's Rd

This tour can be done easily by underground or bus and on foot – it
takes in most of the length of the King's Rd and New King's Rd, fast
becoming the discount centre of London. The nearest underground
station to the start is Sloane Square. From here it is only a few minutes
walk to our first stop the **Joseph Clearance shop** at 53 Kings Rd. Here

you will find end of season and clearance lines from the Joseph label at tempting reductions of up to 70%. Don't worry if you find nothing to entice you here as there are more opportunities further up the road including the Designer Sample Store at no. 289 and some opportunistic short-lease shops offering designer discounts.

First, however, if you are in the mood for sightseeing, take a left down Smith St and keep going until you meet Royal Hospital Rd. Turn right up this road and on your left you will find the **National Army Museum.** This houses some fabulous reconstructions that enable you to see how soldiers lived and fought from Tudor times to the present day. Exhibits include uniforms, weapons, equipment, paintings, models and all manner of interesting items in one of the most superb collections of its kind in the world.

From here you are very close to **Carlyle's House** at 24 Cheyne Row (see map) which is only 4 or 5 minutes walk away. The Victorian essayist and thinker lived in this 18th century house from 1834 until his death in 1881 and it has been preserved very much as he and his family lived in it with much of the original decoration and furniture. Here Chopin played at the piano and Carlyle conversed with such literary acquaintances as Alfred Lord Tennyson and William Thackeray. Visiting the house is to re-visit the Victorian era he lived in.

If you return via Oakley Rd to Kings Rd at the junction you will not be far from No. 201 which is the site of **Designers Sale Studio.** Here you will find catwalk clothes for both women and men at discounts of up to 60%. Perfectly tailored Armani, Bagutta and Apara suits and separates hang alongside pastel shades in chiffon by Genny, together with the essential military pinstripe from Complice. Also available are designer bodies, T-shirts and jeans from Emporio Armani and Dolce e Gabbana as well as accessories by Moschino and Genny and the indispensable Prada handbag.

To round off your shopping you should not miss the opportunity to visit the **VIVM shop** at 201 New Kings Rd into which Kings Rd runs. This stylish shop at the Parsons Green end of the New King's Road offers fabulous new designer clothes and accessories at substantial discounts - usually half the original price. The clothes are as impressive as the decor, with outfits from Caroline Charles, Maxfield Parrish, Paddy Campbell, Robinson Valentine, Edina Ronay, Ungaro, Sonja Nuttall, Paul Frith's elegant evening wear, Pazuki's waistcoats and silk dressing gowns, Alfred Dunhill and Lesley George. The shop also sells handbags from Lulu Guinness, scarves from Harriet Anstruther and Jan Lindsay, and jewellery from Reema Pachachi, painted shirts from Carole Waller and silk shoes from Orford and Swan. Owner Micola Nevile has many contacts in the top end of the fashion industry and is supplied direct from the designers with returned orders, samples and end of season outfits. There are also some menswear gift items from Alfred Dunhill such as ties, braces, cashmere scarves and sweaters - all at half the original price.

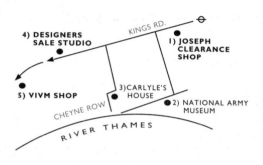

FACTFILE

1) Joseph Clearance Shop
53 KING'S RD, LONDON SW3
TEL: 0171 730 7562
Open 10.30am - 6.30pm Monday - Saturday, 10.30am - 7pm, Wednesday, 12 noon - 5pm Sunday.

2) The National Army Museum
ROYAL HOSPITAL RD, CHELSEA, LONDON SW3 4HT
TEL: 0171 730 0717
Open: All year, daily 10am - 5.30pm (closed Good Friday, May Day, 24th, 25th December and 1st January). Admission: Free

3) Carlyle's House
24 CHEYNE ROW, LONDON SW3 5HL
TEL: 0171 352 7087
Open: April - end of October, Wednesday -Sun day and Bank Holiday Mondays 11am - 5pm last Admission 4.30pm (closed Good Friday) Admission: Adults £3, children £1.50, National Trust members free.

4) Designer's Sale Studio

201 KING'S RD, LONDON SW3 5EL
TEL: 0171 351 4171
Open 10.30am - 6.30pm Monday - Friday, 10am - 6pm Saturday,
12 noon - 6pm Sunday

4) The Designer Sample Store

289 KING'S RD, LONDON SW3 5EW
TEL: 0171 351 0880
Open 10.30am - 6.30pm Monday - Saturday.

5) VIVM

201 NEW KING'S RD, LONDON SW6 4SR
TEL: 0171 731 5567
Open 10am - 6pm Monday - Saturday, 10am - 7pm Wednesday

TOUR 4
Waltham Abbey, Harlow, Nazeing, Hatfield House and Hemel Hempstead

This tour takes in an area of Essex and Hertfordshire on the outskirts of north and northeast London. In this area there is a cluster of new and old-established towns mixed with rural villages. The area is very much a part of the London commuter belt but nevertheless there are some attractive stretches of countryside and some sights with wonderful historic connections

The tour starts at **Waltham Abbey** in Essex where, only 16 miles or so from the heart of London, is one of the best surviving examples of Norman architecture in the country. Building work actually began prior to the Conquest but the great nave is 12th century Norman and is part of what survives today. The present church of The Holy Cross and St Lawrence contains 19th century stained glass windows wrought by Sir Edward Burne-Jones. In the Lady Chapel is the remains of a 14th century painting on the east wall over the Altar.

A short drive up the B194 will then take you to Broxbourne where **Nazeing Glass** is situated at Nazeing New Rd. This has a large factory shop measuring almost 2,000 sq ft selling seconds, overmakes and ends of lines from a range of cut glass decanters, rose bowls, vases, and jugs. They also sell champagne flutes, liqueur and cocktail glasses at factory shop prices, which in practice means 20%-40% off. There are 20 different suites of wine glass in seven different sizes.

A short drive east via Nazeing will then take you to Harlow, not normally a town to figure on the tourist maps, but significant to this book as the site of the **Sterling Leathers factory shop.** Sterling Leathers manufacture top quality women's and men's leather and suede garments for many of the best known names at the upper end of the high street. Their production ranges from full-length coats, jackets and blousons to waistcoats. Their factory shop at Harlow is a bargain hunter's paradise which sells garments a good deal cheaper than normal retail prices.

From Harlow a drive of around 20 miles west along the A414 will take you to the A1000 on which a short drive south will bring you to **Hatfield House,** one of the great country houses of England. A huge Jacobean mansion built in 1607 now stands near the site of the old palace where Elizabeth 1 and Mary Tudor were both held in virtual captivity during their childhoods. Little now remains of the old palace apart from the Great Hall and a few other rooms but the new house contains much in the way of historic connections with "the Virgin Queen". The superb park and gardens include a parterre, a scented garden and knot garden with plants typical of the 15th to 17th centuries.

Having broken your journey at Hatfield why not press on westwards along the A414 and M10 to Hemel Hempstead where, at the Maylands Wood Estate you can call in at the **Aquascutum factory shop.** Here you will find previous season's stock and seconds for women and men at greatly reduced prices. For men, blazers, suits and silk ties. Examples include 60% off men's suits and half-price ladies silk blouses.

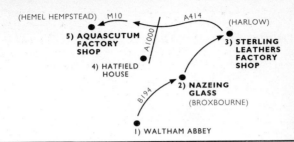

FACTFILE

1) Waltham Abbey
OFF A112, ESSEX.
Open: At reasonable times. Admission: Free

2) Nazeing Glass Works Ltd.
NAZEING NEW ROAD, BROXBOURNE, HERTFORDSHIRE EN10 6SU
TEL: 01992 464485
Open: 9.30am - 4.30pm Monday - Friday, 9.30am - 3pm Saturday

3) Sterling Leathers
UNIT A2, SEEDBED CENTRE, COLDHARBOUR ROAD, PINNACLES,
HARLOW, ESSEX CM19 5AF
TEL: 01279 444449
Open: 9am - 4pm Monday - Fri,day 10am - 12 noon Saturday

4) Hatfield House
HATFIELD, HERTFORDSHIRE AL9 5NQ
TEL: 01707 262823
Open: 25th March to the 2nd Sunday in October, **House:** Tuesday -
Saturday 12 noon - 4pm, Sunday 1.00pm - 4.30pm, Bank Holidays
11am - 5pm, Park: 10.30am - 8pm **Gardens** 11am - 6pm daily.
Admission: House, Park & Gardens £5 .20 (children £3.30, OAPs
£4.40), Park, Gardens and Exhibitions £2.90 (children £2.20, OAPs
£2.70). 20 or more people please book in advance.

5) Aquascutum
CLEVELAND ROAD, MAYLANDS WOOD ESTATE, HEMEL
HEMPSTEAD, HERTFORDSHIRE HP2 7EY
TEL: 01442 248333
Open: 10am - 4pm Monday - Saturday.

TOUR 5

Nyman's Garden, Burgess Hill, Hickstead, Ditchling Beacon, Merchants Quay

Our tour starts at **Nymans Garden,** West Sussex on the B2114 at Handcross. Begun by Ludwig Messel in 1885, this is one of the great gardens of the south of England full of all sorts of rare plants, shrubs and trees from all over the world. There is a walled garden, a hidden sunken garden and romantic ruins. Sometimes musical evenings are held here in the summer for which the setting is perfect.

A six mile drive south from here down the A23 takes you to Hickstead the home of **M&G Designer Fashions.** This is a large fashion warehouse selling designer and famous high-street name clothes at discounted prices from 20% to 80% less than the normal retail price. Because they carry many famous high street and designer labels in the 3,400 sq ft outlet, they are unable to advertise these names. Some of the clothes are discontinued lines, others late deliveries, bankrupt stock or cancelled orders. Twice a year, they hold "silly" sales where no garment is over £30. They also hold winter and summer clearance sales. Their range covers everything from T-shirts to ballgowns in sizes 10-28. There is ample parking, free coffee or tea, easy access for wheelchairs and indi- vidual changing rooms. They have only recently started selling menswear, mens and ladies shoes. (Follow the signs to Ricebridge and Hickstead Village.)

Next make your way east across minor country roads to Burgess Hill. Here at 208 London Rd is the **Jaeger factory shop** which provides classic tailoring from Jaeger, Jaeger Man and Viyella at old-fashioned prices for women and men. Most of the merchandise is last season's stock and there are some seconds, but you may find the odd gem from this season if you hunt carefully. This shop sells mens and ladies wear, as well as accessories, towels and linens.

Hopefully clutching a bargain buy, go and relax at the National Trust maintained **Ditchling Beacon** which is about 5 miles south of here down the B2112 finally turning off onto a minor road. Here, on the ridge of the South Downs there is the remains of a hill-fort and from the car park there is a splendid view across the Weald. When the sky is clear the view extends as far as the North Downs.

From here it is just a short hop to Brighton Marina where there is the

Merchants Quay factory shopping village. Here there are ten main factory shops including The Factory Shop, Tom Sayer menswear, Edinburgh Crystal, Bookscene, Honey fashions and Hornsea Pottery. The Options Shopping Mall, which leads from the Factory Shop, contains twenty-four small factory concessions including James Barry, Dannimac, Double Two shirts, Alexara and Selfridges. There is also a gift shop called Sanctuary Cove, a framing shop, a full-price bridal shop, a multiplex 8-screen cinema, an Asda superstore, small playground and a variety of eating places including the new Mcdonalds Drive Thru and Hanrahan's Irish/American theme pub. Further shops are planned for 1997.

FACTFILE

1) Nymans Garden
HANDCROSS, WEST SUSSEX
TEL: 01444 400321
Open: March - October, daily (ex Monday and Tuesday) but open Bank Holiday Monday 11am - 7pm or sunset if earlier. Last admission 1 hour before closing. Admission: £4.20 (family ticket £10) parties £3.50

2) M & G Designer Fashions
OLD LONDON ROAD (OLD A23), HICKSTEAD VILLAGE, WEST SUSSEX RH17 5RL
TEL: 01444 881511.
Open: 10am - 5pm Monday - Saturday and some Bank Holidays; telephone first.

3) The Jaeger Factory Shop
208 LONDON RD, BURGESS HILL, WEST SUSSEX RH15 9RD
TEL: 01444 871123
Open: 12.30pm - 4pm Monday 9.30 am - 4pmTuesday - Friday,
9.30am - 3.30pm Saturday.

4) The Ditchling Beacon
NR DITCHLING WEST SUSSEX
Open: All year round. Admission: Free

5) Merchants Quay Factory Shopping Village
BRIGHTON MARINA, BRIGHTON, EAST SUSSEX BN2 5UF
TEL: 01273 693636. FAX 01273 675082
Opening Times: 10am - 5.30pm. 10am - 5pm Sunday, during
January, February, March. Hours to be extended during the summer
months.

TOUR 6
Lamberhurst, Cranbrook and Battle

This tour starts at **A Barn Full of Sofas and Chairs** based at Furnace
Mill, Lamberhurst. Here there are three storeys of pre-1950s sofas and
chairs, some antique, ranging from £200-£400. If you like (and you are
willing to pay for it!) they can restore them back to their original state
using all the traditional fabrics or you can buy them in an un-restored
condition. They also sell new ranges of sofas based on old models from
£1,600 upwards.

Just south of Lamberhurst, off the A21, is one of Britain's most
romantic sights: **Scotney Castle and Gardens.** Here, nestling in a
wooded valley, there is a ruined 16th century manor house surrounded
by a moat and the most glorious gardens. Azaleas, roses and rhododen-
drons abound and whatever time of year you visit there is something to
see.

From here, if you retrace your steps slightly via the A21 northbound
and the A262 and make your way to Cranbrook, you will find on the
High St **Bell House Fabrics.** This two-storey shop makes browsing and
buying a pleasure. Sanderson specialists, they also operate an ordering
service for other manufacturers, too, at competitive prices. They carry

current, seconds and discontinued lines, priced appropriately. Most printed cottons cost from £4.99 to £9.99; brocades from £9.99 - £11.99. There are also tapestries, damasks and dress fabrics from £1.25 a metre for dress nets and £8 a metre for silks. They also sell new upholstered furniture and operate a full interior design service.

From here take the A229 and A268 to **Rye,** one of the most picturesque towns in England with its wealth of medieval, Tudor, Stuart and Georgian houses. Just walking around the town is a pleasure but if you want to know something of the town's history go to the **Museum** housed in the Ypres Tower. Here there are displays on local history, along with examples of Rye Pottery and displays relating to Rye's maritime history and that of the other Cinque Ports.

Rye Pottery, of course, is still going strong and the factory shop can be visited at 77 Ferry Rd. There is always a selection of seconds available in distinctive hand-decorated designs. No two items of this 'majolica' or 'delft' decorated pottery are the same, which is why it is still popular with the Royal Family. Choose from Chaucer figures, American folk heroes, scenes from Alice or Pastoral Primitives; seconds are usually two-thirds of retail price.

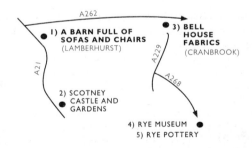

FACTFILE

1) A Barn Full of Sofas and Chairs

FURNACE MILL, LAMBERHURST, KENT TN3 8LH
TEL: 01892 890285
Open 10am - 5pm Tuesday - Saturday

2) Scotney Castle Garden,

LAMBERHURST, KENT TN3 8JN
TEL: 01892 890651
Garden Open: April - October, Old Castle Open 1st May-11th
September , Wednesday - Friday 11am - 6pm, Saturday and Sunday
2pm - 6pm or sunset if earlier. Bank Holiday Mondays 12 noon -
6pm (closed Good Friday) last admission 1 hr before closing
Admission: £3.50 (children £1.80).

3) Bell House Fabrics

HIGH ST, CRANBROOK, KENT. TN17 3DN
TEL: 01580 712555
Open: 9am - 5.30pm Monday - Saturday.
Closed Wednesday afternoons

4) Rye Museum

RYE CASTLE, GUN GARDEN, EAST SUSSEX
TEL: 01797 226728
Open: Easter-October, daily 10.30am 5.30pm (last admission 30 mins
before close). November - March most weekends 11.30am - 3.30pm.
Admission: £1.50 (OAPs £1 Children under16 50p) NB. This attraction will be closed for at least 1 year from October1995 for necessary
repairs to the tower.

5) Rye Pottery

77 FERRY ROAD, RYE, EAST SUSSEX. TN31 7DJ
TEL: 01797 223363
Open: 9am - 5pm Monday - Saturday,
Closed 12.30 noon - 2pm Daily.

THE SOUTH WEST

Our three tours in the south west of England take us through some of the most charming by-ways of Old Wessex – that part of England in which the hard-pressed Saxons of Alfred's time took their final stand against the Danish invaders, withstood their onslaught and lived to form an impregnable barrier against their further depredations. It is a part of the country where the sense of time gone by, of being just a modern expression of an ancient civilization is almost palpable. Salisbury Plain, Glastonbury, the winding lanes of Dorset may all look different but have an ancient atmosphere that is one and the same.

TOUR 1
Breamore House, Downton, Odstock, Wilton, Warminster and Stonehenge

Breamore House lies just north of Breamore on the A338 and is a red brick Elizabethan manor house that was completed in 1583 just five years before the Spanish Armada set sail. Although there was a fire in 1857, the structure emerged unscathed and the house, which has been in the ownership of the Hulse family for over 200 years, contains an impressive collection of paintings, china and tapestries. There is also a museum in the grounds which houses coaches and steam engines and other exhibits which illustrate how people lived and worked in times past.

From here a short trip north up the A338 takes you to the village of Downton where you can undergo one of the most unexpected shopping experiences in the British Isles. In this remote rural hideaway is based the **Downton Trading Company** where Bryn Parry, cartoonist and frame maker to the White House, has opened a shop selling other top-name small company's seconds, overmakes, discounted and discontinued lines. The number of companies changes constantly but there are usually about 40 or 50 selling different goods in the shop at any one time, with a changeover of stock every three months.

This pot pourri of high quality products includes hand-painted porcelain boxes; hand-lacquered tablemats, trays and wastepaper baskets; tapestry stools; limited edition paintings and prints; drawing room china; seconds in high quality photograph frames, clocks, cartoon frames, and greetings cards from Bryn Parry; oleographs; designer fabric nursery bags; and silk ties and braces; as well as candles, leather goods, table lamps and shades, drawing room furniture, plant pot holders, silver for the dining room table, American soft toys, conservatory furniture and accessories, kitchen pottery, leather-bound photograph albums, bulletin boards, Christmas decorations (in season), crystal glass and Victorian paintings.

Everything is colour coded in four categories so you can tell whether you're buying a second, discounted, overmake or a perfect but discontinued line, and prices reflect that. The shop is situated in the centre of the village next to the tannery.

Next stop (avoiding the lunch hour 1-2 when it is closed), if you're interested in high quality designer fashion accessories, is **Georgina von Etzdorf's** small but characterful factory shop on the outskirts of Odstock only 4 miles north of Downton just off the A338. Sandwiched between workrooms , it has a limited but exciting range of clothes and lots of wonderful accessories. Her products are not cheap, but the jacquard scarves, squares and shawls, and the men's silk cravats, ties and jacquard silk scarves with cashmere linings are affordable at prices ranging from £20. Everything is half price, which means that the lovely devore tunic jackets, which cost £385 in the shops are marked down to £181 here. The price tag also tells you what season the outfit is from and whether it is a second. There are men's silk dressing gowns at about £200, georgette long and short dresses, £170 and £193, wool crepe long gloves, £25, ladies jacquard print waistcoats, £88, men's silk cravats, £21.50, silk ties, from £10, and oddments of fabric.

A further 5 miles skirting around Salisbury and out west on the A30 will bring you to **Wilton House** with its many acres of landscaped parkland, woodland and water gardens. The house itself, the seat of the Earls of Pembroke, is largely a magnificent creation of the 17th century architect Inigo Jones and boasts superb painted ceilings, a world famous art collection, a reconstructed Tudor kitchen and the estate's original Victorian laundry.

If it's spring or early autumn and more shopping appeals to you then, after Wilton, retrace your steps to the A36 and head about 20 miles west to Warminster. Here, on Fairfield Rd, you will find the factory shop of **Dents,** the accessories company, which produces such covetable gloves, belts, handbags, leather wallets and purses for most of the big department stores. Most of the stock in this reasonably-sized warehouse shop consists of gloves, sold at at least 50% discount, but there are also some umbrellas, including telescopic, golf and walking umbrellas, handbags, silk ties, leather belts, leather card holders and key fobs. Stock from the discontinued lines and end of ranges changes constantly. The shop usually closes for the summer between May and September so phone first to check it is open.

Warminster lies on the western edge of Salisbury Plain and being so close it would be unforgiveable not to visit one of Europe's greatest pre-historic sites at **Stonehenge.** A journey of about 16 miles eastwards via the A36, A303 and A360 will take you to the site through the vast rather rather eerie plain on which the henge sits. It is always a challenge to the imagination of any visitor how primitive men over three thousand years ago could have managed to quarry these vast stones, transport them and then erect them in a manner and pattern that for centuries has provoked all manner of speculation as to its purpose. Go and see for yourself – you may come up with the answer!

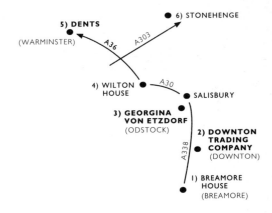

FACTFILE

1) Breamore House
COUNTRYSIDE & CARRIAGE MUSEUMS, BREAMORE, HAMPSHIRE
TEL: 01725 512468
Open: April Tuesday, Wednesday and Sunday 2pm - 5.30pm,
May- July and September Tuesday - Thursday, Saturday and Sunday
and Bank Holidays 2pm - 5.30pm, August daily 2pm - 5.30pm
Admission: £4.50 (children £3.00)

2) The Downton Trading Company
THE OLD MANSION HOUSE, 3 THE HIGH STREET, DOWNTON ,
NR SALISBURY, WILTSHIRE SP5 3PG.
TEL: 01725 510676
Open: 9.30-am - 5pm Monday - Saturday

3) The Georgina von Etzdorf Factory Shop
THE AVENUE, ODSTOCK, NEAR SALISBURY, WILTSHIRE.
TEL: 01722 326625.
Open: 10am - 6pm Monday - Saturday, 12 noon - 5pm Sunday
(closed 1pm - 2pm for lunch daily)

4) Wilton House
WILTON, NR SALISBURY, WILTSHIRE SP2 0BJ
TEL: 01722 743115
Open: 3rd April - 3rd November daily 11am - 6pm
Admission: £6.20 (children 5-15 £3.80 OAPs and Students £5.20)

5) Dents Factory Shop
FAIRFIELD RD, WARMINSTER, WILTSHIRE BA12 9DL.
TEL: 01985 212291.
Open: 10am - 4pm Tuesday - Saturday.
Telephone first to check opening hours.

6) Stonehenge
AMESBURY, WILTSHIRE (OFF THE A360)
TEL: 01980 625368/INFORMATION LINE 01980 624715
Open: 361 days per year, 16th March - 31st May 9.30am - 6pm, 1st
June - 31st August 9am - 7pm. 1st September - 15th October 9.30am
- 6pm, 16th October - 15th March 1997 9.30am - 4pm (closed 24th,
25th, 26th December and 1st January). Admission: £3.50 (children 5
- 15 years £1.80, OAPs and Students £2.60) 10% discount for groups
of 11 people or more.

TOUR 2
Shepton Mallet, Wells, Street and Glastonbury

Our tour starts in **Wells,** England's smallest cathedral city, where the
12th and 13th century cathedral provides a glorious example of English
Gothic. With a population barely double what it was in medieval times,
the city has preserved much of its ancient and ecclesiastical atmosphere.
Near to the cathedral is the moated bishop's palace where the state
rooms and gallery are well worth a visit, access being through the 14th

century gatehouse. Inside the palace grounds are the ancient wells from which the city derives its name.

From Wells a drive of around 5 miles along the A371 takes you to Shepton Mallet where the town church has an intricately carved barrel ceiling – one of the finest in the West Country – and an equally fine carved stone pulpit. However, the chief attraction here for us lies in the Old School House, Kilver Street where is to be found the factory shop for **Mulberry's** famous leather goods.

Situated on the Yeovil to Glastonbury Road, off the A361, outside Shepton Mallet, this popular, large and attractive factory outlet sells last season's and slightly substandard items from the famous Mulberry leather handbags, briefcases, filofaxes and wallets at discounted prices. The new factory shop (they moved from Chilcompton in August 1995) is sufficiently large to also display ends of lines from the homes range of sofas, fabrics, occasional tables, lamps, rugs, throws, cushions, china, decanters and glass. Also there are rails of last season's clothes including men's jackets, waxed jackets, trousers, shirts, waistcoats, braces and shoes; and women's jackets, handknitted sweaters and cardigans, jackets and coats. There are also umbrellas, pewter napkin rings, golfing and fishing gifts, shaving kits, and a skincare range. Discontinued lines are discounted by 30%-40%; current seconds, many of which come direct from the factory, are discounted by 20%.

A 15 minute drive along the A361 westwards will then take you on to **Glastonbury,** the seat of much Arthurian legend where under a spring on the slopes of the Tor Joseph of Arimathea is supposed to have buried the holy grail – the chalice used by Christ at the Last Supper. King Arthur and his Queen Guinevere are said to have been buried at Glastonbury and the medieval abbey (now an atmospheric ruin) was a place of regular pilgrimage in the Middle Ages. The superb view from the Tor over Glastonbury, Wells and the Bristol Channel makes its ascent almost compulsory.

It is a short hop west from here along the A361 to a unique and exciting shopping experience at the **Clark's Factory Shopping Village** in Street. You should leave plenty of time for this as there is so much to see. Clark's is a purpose-built village of brick-built shops with extensive car parking facilities. Other facilities include a restaurant run by Leith's, fast food stands, carousel, an indoor play area and an outdoor play area. Here, in addition to the C&J Clark's factory shop where many bargain buys are to be had, there are another 36 shops with more planned: Royal Brierley, Royal Worcester, Denby Pottery, Dartington Crystal, Jumpers,

Monsoon/Accessorize, Laura Ashley, Benetton, Crabtree & Evelyn, The Baggage Factory, The Linen Cupboard, The Pier, Wrangler, James Barry, Jaeger, Viyella, Alexon/Eastex/Dash, Fred Perry, Triumph, JoKids, Claude Gill Books, Woolea (which also sells Lyle & Scott and Barbour), Rohan, Farah Menswear, Thorntons Chocolates, The Sports Factory, Windsmoor (which also sells Planet, Berkertex, Precis and Genesis), Black & Decker, Liz Claiborne, Hallmark, Remington, Tridias children's toys and Esprit.

There is also The Shoe Museum which contains shoes from Roman times to the present day along with machinery, hand tools, fashion plates and engravings

If this isn't enough to blunt your shopping appetite there is one more shopping experience nearby to savour – the **Morlands Sheepskin factory shop.** Manufacturers in the same area for 120 years, Morlands has a factory shop near Glastonbury on the A29. It sells traditional sheepskin coats from £199, leather jackets, boots, suede waistcoats from £39.99, hats, moccasins, rugs, slippers and gloves. Stock is mostly for men with some children's sizes. Most are seconds or overstock.

FACTFILE

1) Wells Cathedral

WELLS, SOMERSET
TEL: 01749 674483
Open: Every day 7.15am - 6pm; July and August open until 8.30pm.
Admission: £1 for pre-booked guided tours. Suggested voluntary donations of £3 per adult and £2.50 per person for a party of 10 or more to visit the Cathedral

2) The Bishop's Palace
WELLS, SOMERSET
TEL: 01749 678691
Open: 2nd April - 30th October, Tuesday, Thursday & Bank Holiday
Monday; daily in August 11am - 6pm, Sun 2pm - 6pm

3) The Mulberry Factory Shop
THE OLD SCHOOL HOUSE, KILVER STREET, SHEPTON MALLET,
SOMERSET, BA4 5NF (ON A37)
TEL: 01749 340583.
Open 10am - 6pm Monday - Saturday, 11am - 4pm Sunday.

4) Glastonbury Abbey
GLASTONBURY, SOMERSET
TEL: 01458 832267
Open: all year daily. June to August 9am - 6pm; September - May
9.30am - dusk or 6pm whichever is earlier. Closed Christmas day.
Admission: £2.50 (children £1, students and OAPs £2, family ticket 2
adults and 2 children under 16 years £5.50)

5) Clark's Factory Shopping Village
FARM RD, STREET, SOMERSET. BA16 OBB
TEL: 01458 840064.
Open 9am - 5.30pm Monday - Saturday, from April 1st closed at
6pm, Monday - Saturday, 11am - 5pm Sunday.
Larger shops not open on Easter Sunday

6) The Shoe Museum
C & J CLARK LTD, HIGH STREET, STREET, SOMERSET
TEL: 01458 443131
Open: all year daily 10am - 4.45pm Monday - Friday, 10am - 5pm
Saturday, 11am - 5pm Sunday: Closed 25th and 26th December and
1st January Admission free

7) Morlands, Sheepskin Factory Shop
NORTHOVER, NR GLASTONBURY, SOMERSET.
TEL: 01458 835042
Open 9.30am - 5pm Monday - Friday, 9.30am - 4.45pm Saturday

Tour 3
Poole, Kingston Lacy, Sturminster Newton and Sherborne

Poole Pottery located on the Quay at Poole continues a 1,700-year-old tradition of pottery in this area and combines both entertainment and excellent bargain shopping opportunities. There is a factory tour, a 'have a go' area, glass blowing, a display of past and present pottery, a craft village and a factory shop selling seconds and some perfects including Stuart Crystal, Dartington Crystal, Colony Candles and Henry Watson terracotta at discounts of about 30%. The Poole Pottery selection includes their most popular ranges: Dorset Fruit in four variations (orange, plum apple and pear), the Vineyard range and Vincent, the sunflower range, all with matching textiles. Giftware includes the famous blue dolphins, large storage jars, bread crocks and butter boxes.

From here you might want to drop in at the **Waterfront Museum** situated amongst medieval buildings at 4, High St, The Quay, where you can witness the full story of Poole's seafaring past. Otherwise, you can head straight out on the A349 and B3082 about 8 miles to **Kingston Lacy House** on the outskirts of Wimborne. This fine house was built during the 17th century but later transformed by its 19th century owner into a superb reproduction of an Italian palazzo. Treasures from all over Europe were brought here and its art collection is quite outstanding with works by Rubens, Titian, Velazquez and Reynolds. The National Trust now owns the house and the 1,500 acres of parkland and garden that can be visited separately to the house if time is pressing

A journey about 16 miles further west on the A357 past Blandford Forum will take you to the premises in Sturminster Newton of **Hansons Discount Fabrics.** Fashion and curtain fabric specialists, they also sell sewing machines, haberdashery, craft items, and patterns. They stock all the well-known names such as Rose & Hubble, James Hare, Bennett silks, Liberty and Ibor, and the full range of fabric weights. There is lots of choice for wedding dress fabric: polyester dupion, satin, silk dupion, taffeta, tuiles, veiling and lining. There is no making-up service for brides but lots of bridal pattern books available. If you spend more than £25, you get a 5% discount; more than £125 and you receive a seven and a half percent discount; more than £250 and your discount is 10%.

Sewing machines are very competitively priced.

Another 15 to 20 minutes west along the same road will take you to the medieval town of **Sherborne** with its famous 15th century abbey housing two famous schools and its two castles, the Old and the New. Both castles are open to the public. The old was built in the 12th century but captured and destroyed by Cromwell's forces during the civil war. There now remains the ruins of the main buildings, the curtain walls towers and gates. Between this and the new castle that were both at one time owned by Sir Walter Raleigh lies an artificial lake designed by 'Capability' Brown. The new castle is a 16th century house which contains paintings, porcelain, fine furniture and many items of historical interest.

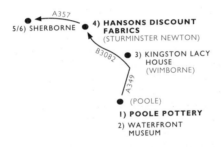

FACTFILE

I) Poole Pottery
THE QUAY, POOLE, DORSET. BH15 1RF
TEL: 01202 666200
Open: 9am - 5pm Monday - Saturday, 10am - 5pm Sunday. Times of opening change from 1st April. Factory Tours: 10am - 4pm Monday - Thursday, 10am - 12.30pm Friday.
Admission £2.50 (children £1.50, OAPs £2, family ticket £6.50)
Groups of more than 10 people £1.50 each

2) Waterfront Museum
4 HIGH STREET, POOLE, DORSET
TEL: 01202 683138
Open: All year Monday - Saturday 10am - 5pm, Sunday 2pm - 5pm
(closed Good Friday, 25th and 26th December and 1st January Times
of opening are changeable during summer months. Admission:
October - March, £1.50 (children 90p OAPs and students £1.30)
family ticket £5. April, June and September, £1.95 (children £1.25,
OAPs and students £1.75) family ticket £7. July - August £2.50
(children £1.75, OAPs and students £2.30) family ticket £8.25.
10% discount on group rate of 10 or more people.

3) Kingston Lacy House
GARDEN & PARK, NR WIMBORNE, DORSET
TEL: 01202 883402
Open: April to 31st October daily, except Thursday and Friday, 12
noon - 5.30pm. Park & Garden 11.30am to 6pm. Last admission to
house 4.30pm. Admission: to house, garden and park £5.50 (children
£2.70), to garden and park £2.20 (children £1.10).
No concessions for OAPs

4) Hansons Discount Fabrics
OLD STATION YARD, STATION RD, STURMINSTER NEWTON,
DORSET.
TEL: 01258 472698.
Open: 9am - 5.30pm Monday - Saturday, until 7pm on Friday.

5) Sherborne Old Castle
SHERBORNE, DORSET
TEL: 01935 812730
Phone first for opening details and cost of admission.

6) Sherborne New Castle
SHERBORNE, DORSET
TEL: 01935 813182
Open: Easter to September, Thursday, Saturday, Sunday and Bank
Holidays. Admission: Adults £3.60 (Children £1.80, OAPs £3.00)

THE COTSWOLDS

This area in the south west midlands of England contains some of the loveliest countryside and most charming villages and towns in the whole of the British Isles. Impossibly pretty cottages with beautifully-tended gardens, stone-built in honey-coloured limestone characterise the Cotswold area that runs from Banbury in the east to Cheltenham and Bath in the west. There are wonderful views to be had from the roads that run along the high limestone ridge of small towns and villages nestling comfortably in the valleys cut by such rivers as the Windrush and Evenlode. There are grand houses and sites of great historical interest and, in addition to this, there are factory shops and outlets where some amazing bargains can be picked up during the course of an enjoyable car tour.

TOUR 1
Blenheim Palace and Bicester Village

A few miles north of Oxford on the A44 lies the village of Woodstock which, along with some splendid pubs, boasts one of the greatest historic landscaped houses in Britain, **Blenheim Palace.** This enormous baroque palace, home to the Dukes of Marlborough, is set in over 2000 acres of landscaped parkland and is considered to be one of the architect Vanbrugh's finest works. Certainly, the view that opens up as you pass through the gates at the west end of the village must rate as one of the finest sights in England.

You'll need at least three hours to do the house and grounds justice but after spending the morning there why not travel on to Bicester about twenty minutes away up the A34 (east).

Bicester Shopping Village, which opened in June 1995, comprises 48 different outlets. Billed as 'Bond Street comes to Bicester', the shops are very smart indeed, beautifully designed and stocked with end-of-season designer fashions, mens and childrenswear, tableware, shoes and more, all on permanent sale at prices reduced from 25%-50%, with some reductions up to 75%. The outlets include: casualwear for all the family from Benetton; witty slogans on T-shirts and nightshirts from the US company, Big Dog; Cerruti women's designer fashions; Clarks footwear; sports shoes from the US company, Converse; glassware and crystal from Edinburgh Crystal; brand name luggage from Equator; casualwear and sportswear from Fred Perry; home furnishings from Hico; women's shoes and fashions from high street shop, Hobbs; men's and women's underwear and swimwear from HOM and Triumph; women's shoes and handbags from Jane Shilton; designer fashion from Karen Millen; younger women's fashions from Jeffrey Rogers; men's and women's fashions from Jigsaw; children clothes for boys and girls from JoKids; women's designer shoes and fashions from Joan & David; country clothing from John Partridge; glassware from John Jenkins; footwear from Kurt Geiger; toys and games from well-known names such as Hasbro, Mattel, Matchbox, Little Tikes at Kids Play Factory; specialist outerwear from Mileta Sport at Tog 24; women's fashions from Monsoon; gifts and homes accessories from Museum Merchandise; silver and stainless cutlery from Oneida; childrenswear from Osh Kosh b'Gosh; casualwear from Pepe Jeans; designer fashions for men and women from Polo Ralph Lauren; candles and candlesticks from Price's Candles; men's and women's fashions from Principles; casualwear and after sailing clothes for men and women from Scandinavian company Red/Green; casualwear from mail order specialists Racing Green; books, CDs and cassettes from Sapphire Books; men's and women's fashions from Scotch House; men's suits, jackets and top designer name shirts from the Moss Bros shop, The Suit Company; topclass tableware and glass from Villeroy & Boch; lingerie from Warners; toiletries and gifts from Woods of Windsor; jeans and casualwear from Wrangler; bedlinen from Descamps; smart women's fashion from Aquascutum and Jaeger; and outdoor clothing from Helly Hansen. The centre also has two restaurants, a small children's play area and free parking.

If you've got any time, energy or spending power left after this experience you can round off the day with a fifteen minute drive up the B4030 to the great Jacobean mansion of **Rousham House** with its wonderfully landscaped gardens overlooking the river Cherwell. Remember to check the opening times in the Factfile.

From Rousham, which you can adequately take in in an hour, it's only five minutes drive to the **Fired Earth factory shop** in Middle Aston. Fired Earth sell seconds and discontinued ranges of tiles, fabric and natural fibre floor coverings. A recently converted stone barn adds the facility of a spacious rug warehouse where kelims, gabbehs and other forms of tribal weaving can be viewed at leisure. Terracotta and slate floor tiles are sold from around £12.50 a square metre upwards and some glazed tiles from around £7.50 a square metre. Typical bargains in fabric range from prototype tartans (unique because they have not been put into production) to slightly soiled crewel works (which simply needs dry cleaning) often at less than cost price. Fired Earth also produce the V&A range of historic and traditional paints and dented paints tins are sold at a discount alongside other "bruised" accessories.

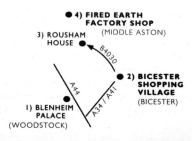

FACTFILE

1) Blenheim Palace

WOODSTOCK, OXFORDSHIRE

TEL: 01993 811091 AND 811325

Open: Palace and Gardens Mid-March to 31st October Monday–
Sunday inclusive 10.30am to 5.30pm (last admission 4.45pm)
Admission Cost: Adults: £7.30, Children (5 to15 years): £3.70, under
5's free, OAPs and students £5.30

2) Bicester Village

PINGLE DRIVE, BICESTER, OXFORDSHIRE OX6 7WD

TEL: 01869 323200

Open All year round except Christmas Day Monday – Sunday
inclusive 10am to 6pm, times of opening may vary during summer
months.

3) Rousham House

STEEPLE ASTON, OXFORDSHIRE

Gardens Open Daily 10.00am to 4.30pm all year
House Open: Wednesdays and Sundays, April to September and Bank
Holidays 2.00pm to 4.30pm
Admission Cost: Gardens £2.50 House: £2.50

4) Fired Earth

MIDDLE ASTON, OXFORDSHIRE, OX5 3PX

TEL: 01869 347599

Open 9.30am to 5.30pm Monday to Saturday

TOUR 2
Witney and the Windrush Valley

Situated on the A40 west of Oxford, Witney, one of the historic 'wool
towns' of the Cotswolds, is the gateway to some of the finest scenery and
interesting sites in the Cotswolds. In the 18th and 19th centuries the
town was famous throughout the country for its blanket weaving. A lot
of its manufacturers have now disappeared but one, **Early's,** is still going
strong. Their factory shop on the Burford Rd is well worth a visit

stocking, at factory prices, blankets in pure new Merino wool, traditional cellular blankets, new designs in cotton blankets, and, in a myriad selection of colours, economy priced acrylic blankets, baby blankets, patchwork quilted bedspreads, the famous Witney Point blankets, white cotton embroidered bedlinen, printed duvet covers, quilts, cot sheets, pram blankets, table cloths, towels, teacloths, tissue box covers and crochet toppers. Blanket stock is made in the next door factory and depends on what has been ordered from there. There are also some seconds, but most of the goods are perfects. A great place to shop for new bedlinen and bedspreads. There were some exceptional bargains in slightly marked bedspreads and some clearance items when we visited.

Also in Witney and worth a visit is the **Factory Shop** at Newlands – part of the Coats Viyella group which makes clothes for many of the high street department stores. This medium sized factory shop stocks clothes for all the family. For women, swimwear, lambswool long cardigans with V-necks or round necks which looked very good value, jackets, skirts, pyjamas, nightdresses, dressing gowns, opaque tights, blouses and underwear. Stock changes constantly.

Having shopped in Witney what better place to lunch or picnic than old **Minster Lovell** (B4027), situated by the banks of the meandering Windrush river. The atmospheric ruins of the 15th century hall are mantained by English Heritage and the church and half-timbered Swan Inn are also well worth visiting set as they are in one of the prettiest villages in an outstanding area.

From here it's just a short drive up the A40 westwards to **Swinbrook,** another village of quite captivating charm set in the Windrush valley. In the summer months, you may be lucky enough to witness cricket being played at probably the most picturesque ground in the country, set as it is on the banks of the river opposite the old mill.

A couple of miles west of Swinbrook, **Burford** is a fine old town seemingly stuck in the 18th century, such is the effect of its Georgian architecture. It abounds with fine old coaching inns, has a marvellous church and a hoard of interesting antique shops. It also has, right next to the A40 roundabout, **Just Fabrics** which sells quality furnishing fabrics, mostly designer clearance, some regular and some their own range which is woven and dyed for them exclusively. There is normally a huge range in stock at very competitive prices.

From Burford if you want to see some high quality, old-fashioned woollen weaving in action then travel 4 miles south down the A361 to the quaint old village of Filkins where the **Cotswold Woollen Weavers** operates in a huge and handsome barn producing high quality cloth for such clients as Burberry and Paul Costelloe. While there is a factory shop on site selling high quality rugs and garments, it does not sell at discount except during the twice-yearly sales. After visiting the Woollen Weavers ask for directions to **Broughton Poggs** church (in the neighbouring hamlet). This ancient Norman church is well-hidden next to the grounds of Broughton Hall but rewards the effort of finding it.

Heading back north out of Filkins, having phoned first for an appointment, you can stop off at the last house on the left "The Grey House" from where **The Curtain Brokers** operates. The Curtain Brokers is an independently-owned and operated business which takes in, then sells, quality and designer unwanted curtains, bedspreads, blinds and affiliated items. These are sourced from people moving, refurbishing, interior designers and hotels revamping. There is an extensive choice of over 150 pairs ranging from small cottage size windows to 12ft drops and 20ft spans, some unlined to interlined, with pelmets and all the trimmings. Prices range from as little as £10 up to £500. Quality is the keynote and often sets of up to seven pairs can be bought. Curtains may also be taken on trial for twenty-four hours for assessment in situ. Alterations are undertaken and a valuation service is available for those people selling their house and wanting to include the curtains in the sale price. They also have an extremely fast made-to-measure service, using their own supplier of manufacturers' ends of lines, at incredible value.

If you're not interested in curtains but you are in pottery you may wish to make your way back via the village of Aston about 20 minutes drive east of Filkins on the B4449. Situated in in a converted barn next to their workshop, **Jane and Stephen Baughan's factory shop** will sell seconds and overmakes of their hand decorated pottery. The pottery is made using traditional methods of slip-casting and jollying before being decorated by hand using a combination of fresh colours and a wide variety of surface designs. They have also developed their own specialised technique of hand stencilling on pottery. Designs range from Sunflower and Blue Wild Clematis to birds and animals and all products are microwave and dishwasher safe.

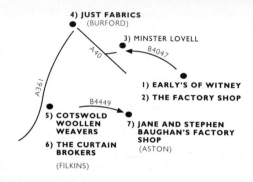

4) JUST FABRICS
(BURFORD)

3) MINSTER LOVELL

B4047

A40

A361

1) EARLY'S OF WITNEY

2) THE FACTORY SHOP

B4449

5) COTSWOLD
WOOLLEN
WEAVERS

7) JANE AND STEPHEN
BAUGHAN'S FACTORY
SHOP
(ASTON)

6) THE CURTAIN
BROKERS

(FILKINS)

FACTFILE

1) Early's of Witney
WITNEY MILL, BURFORD ROAD, WITNEY, OXFORDSHIRE
OX8 5EB
TEL: 01993 703131.
Open 10am - 4pm Monday - Friday, 9am - 2pm Saturday.
Telephone to check if open Bank Holidays

2) The Factory Shop
94 NEWLANDS, WITNEY, OXFORDSHIRE, OX8 6JG
TEL: 01993 708338.
Open 10am - 5pm Monday - Saturday

3) Minster Lovell Hall & Dovecote
MINSTER LOVELL, OXFORDSHIRE
TEL: 0117 9750700 REGIONAL OFFICE,
BRISTOL FOR INFORMATION
Open: All Year April to September daily 10am - 6pm
October to March 10am - 4pm Admission: Free

4) Just Fabrics
BURFORD ANTIQUES CENTRE, CHELTENHAM RD, BURFORD,
OXFORDSHIRE, OX18 4JA
TEL: 01993 823391.
Open 9.30am - 5.30pm Monday - Saturday, 2pm - 5pm Sunday

5) The Cotswold Woollen Weavers
FILKINS, NR LECHLADE, GLOS GL7 3JJ
TEL: 01367 860661
Open: 10am - 6pm Monday to Saturday
2pm - 6pm Sundays

6) The Curtain Brokers
THE GREY HOUSE, FILKINS, NR LECHLADE, GLOS GL7 3JA
TEL: 01367 860362.
Open by appointment only, very flexible. Telephone first

7) Jane & Stephen Baughan
THE STABLE, KINGSWAY FARM, ASTON, OXFORDSHIRE, OX18 2BT
TEL: 01993 850960.
Phone for opening times. An approximate guide to opening times is
8am - 6pm on weekdays and 9am - 3pm on Saturdays.

TOUR 3
Bourton-On-The-Water, Cheltenham and Stroud

Pretty stone houses abound in **Bourton-On-The-Water** through which
flows the seemingly ubiquitous River Windrush. The bird sanctuary
and the model village which is a scale reproduction of Bourton itself are
two interesting places to visit.

Having done that there are bargain shopping opportunities to be had
at **Discount China** which can be found on the High St retailing china
and cookware direct from the factories of Staffordshire. Supplies are
sourced from different manufacturers so stock varies according to what
is available at the time, but includes china fancies, beakers, cookware,
planters, Portmeirion cookware and dinner sets.

Another bargain shopping opportunity is to be found near-at-hand at
Warwicks Fabric clearance shop which stocks own label fabric for
curtains and upholstery from £1.50 a metre for end of rolls up to £9.90.
As well as brand name fabrics, they supply linings, heading tapes,
threads, tracks and poles. They also sell some braiding, trim, fringes and
curtain tracks. Their new showroom opened at the end of February
1996 offering even more bargains.

A 20-minute journey down the A429 and A40 will then take you to the attractive spa town of Cheltenham long-famous for its elegant Regency squares and terraces. One of the shopping areas famous for its architecture is Montpellier and it is there that can be found one of the best nearly-new dress agencies in the country. **Toad Hall** at 7 Rotunda Terrace is a large shop on two floors, almost exclusively filled with designer names. This is a top quality shop: Emporio Armani, MaxMara, Chanel, Givenchy, Armani, Caroline Charles, Escada and Nicole Farhi. The ground floor is devoted to daywear and there's lots of it well set out and presented: suits, jackets, trousers, blouses, bags, hats, sweaters, cardigans. Downstairs is an extensive range of evening wear including evening wraps and coats, plus day coats and jackets and a good range of shoes.

From Cheltenham about a twelve mile trip down the A46 will take you to Stroud, on the way passing through some beautiful hill country with panoramic views and the Benedictine Abbey of Prinknash.

On reaching Stroud you should make for **The Factory Shop** where the wide range of discounted goods on sale includes women's, men's and children's clothing and footwear; household textiles, toiletries, hardware, luggage, lighting and bedding, most of which are chainstore and high street brands at discounts of approximately 30%-50%. There are weekly deliveries and brands include all the major stars: Coloroll, Wrangler and Dartington to name just three. Lines are continually changing and few factory shops offer such a variety under one roof. The Stroud branch has recently been extended to take in men's shoes, children's shoes, children's clothes, toys and books. Although most of the labels have been cut out, you can see the remains of Reebok, Aristoc, Jumpers and Selfridges. This is also a good place to buy children's items, glasses, bedlinen and men's clothes and shoes.

Another interesting factory shop belongs to **Purple Fish,** the mail order shoe company, and is situated in Chalford on the outskirts of Stroud. All the shoes are designed by Purple Fish and made in Spain, mostly in leather, though there are some canvas shoes. These shoes are different from most others in that they are very colourful indeed, with examples in dusty pinks, warm yellows, bright reds and even those which are black have contrasting laces. They are made with leather uppers in linings and rubber soles. There are desert boots, clogs, back to school shoes, trainers, toggle boots and Velcro boots. Sizes range up to adult size 8 and there are also adults shoes in the same style as the children's. The shop stocks some full-price items as well as discontinued lines which are discounted and there are "bargain bins" around with shoes for £10 a pair.

Finally, if you have time, you may wish to head south to Wickwar near Wooton Under Edge where **English Country Pottery** has a factory shop on site just down the stairs from where the large range of pottery is made. Each pot is taken through eight traditional processes, before being handpainted and signed by the paintress. Finally, the pattern is sealed under the glaze and fired, making it very durable: oven, dishwasher, microwave and freezer proof. Here, seconds and discontinued ranges from a wide variety of pottery are sold at half price or less. Some of the pottery has been made by special commission for department stores, galleries and mail order companies, some is wholesaled to the independent gift trade. Because of this, and the fact that they design and manufacture their own pottery, the variety of styles is very wide, resulting in a vibrant, individualistic and very English style of pottery. The designs include: Cats, New England which features farmyard animals, Vegetables, Fiji which is very brightly coloured and includes Fish and Toucans, patterned, Wildlife, Tartan, Shells, Summer hydrangea, Tropical fish, Art deco and New England. The range includes mugs, cups and saucers, lamps, egg cups, ash trays, vases, tea pots, condiments and candlesticks. There is also a shop called **Crafts,** in Bath which sells their seconds at discounted prices. Crafts is at 16 Cheap St, Bath; 01225 464397. Open 9.30-5.30 Mon-Sat.

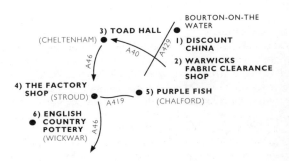

FACTFILE

1) Discount China
HIGH STREET, BOURTON-ON-THE-WATER, NR CHELTENHAM,
GLOUCESTERSHIRE GL54 2AP
TEL: 01451 820662.
Open 11am - 4pm seven days a week during winter months and
10am - 5pm seven days a week during summer months

2) Warwicks Fabrics Clearance Shop
BOURTON-ON-THE-WATER INDUSTRIAL PARK, (JUST OFF A429
STOW TO CIRENCESTER ROAD), BOURTON-ON-THE-WATER,
GLOUCESTERSHIRE GL54 2EN
TEL: 01451 820772.
Open 10am - 5pm Monday - Saturday

3) Toad Hall
THE DRESS AGENCY, 7 ROTUNDA TERRACE, MONTPELLIER,
CHELTENHAM, GLOUCESTERSHIRE GL50 1SW
TEL: 01242 255214.
Open 9am - 5.30pm Monday - Saturday

4) The Factory Shop
CASHES GREEN ROAD RETAIL PARK, OFF WESTWARD ROAD,
CAINSCROSS, STROUD, GLOUCESTERSHIRE GL5 4JE
TEL: 01453 756655.
Open 9am - 5pm Monday - Thursday and Saturday, 9am - 6pm
Friday, 10am - 4pm Sunday and Bank Holidays

5) Purple Fish
THE GATE HOUSE, CHALFORD INDUSTRIAL ESTATE, CHALFORD,
STROUD, GLOUCESTERSHIRE GL6 8NT
TEL: 01453 885010.
Open 9.30am - 5.30pm Monday - Saturday
Mail Order: 01453 882820.

6) English Country Pottery
STATION ROAD, WICKWAR, WOTTON-UNDER-EDGE,
GLOUCESTERSHIRE GL12 8NB
TEL: 01454 299100.
Open 8.30am - 4.30pm Monday - Friday

WALES
SOUTH & NORTH

Mountains and river valleys dominate the splendid scenery in South Wales and are a relevant factor in planning any journey as trips between valleys usually mean journeying north or south to the head or foot of the valley to gain access to the next one. So study your map book well and make generous provisions of time to reach your objectives. But, however long it takes, don't worry as wherever you travel in Wales, north or south, you are guaranteed to pass through some of the most riveting scenery in the British isles where an ancient people clung on to their mountain strongholds resisting successive waves of invaders whilst continuing to preserve their unique language and culture.

TOUR 1
The Rhondda Valley, Treorchy, Cyfarthfa Castle, Blackwood and Caerphilly.

Being in South Wales which for so long was synonymous with coal and choristers makes a visit to the **Rhondda Heritage Park** just off the A470 at Trehafod almost compulsory. Here at the old Lewis Merthyr colliery you can experience the sights, smells and sounds of a colliery at work. There is an underground tour and (above ground but indoors) a recreated village street and period exhibitions which summon up the atmosphere of life in the old fashioned mining communities of the valleys. Other facilities include a restaurant, gift shop and childrens play area.

Our first stop on the shopping tour in South Wales takes us about 10 miles north on the A4058 and A4088 to Treorchy. Here at Ynyswen Rd is situated the factory shop of one of Britain's leading clothes manufacturers, **Burberry.** This shop, although rather olde world, has some top quality merchandise at extremely good prices. It sells seconds and over-makes of the famous name raincoats and duffle coats as well as accessories such as the distinctive umbrellas, scarves and handbags. All carry the Burberry label and are about one third of the normal retail price. For example, trench coats, £159.95; classic coats, £129.95, which amount to a reduction of two thirds. Childrenswear tends to be thin on the ground, but there are plenty of gift items such as Burberry brand name teas, coffees and marmalade.

Having sampled what Burberry has to offer, continuing north on the A4061 will then bring you to the A465 on which you should travel west for Merthyr Tydfil. There are a variety of choices on offer at Merthyr for the cultural tourist. There is the **Cyfarthfa Castle Museum** and **Art Gallery,** a Gothic mansion with beautiful gardens whose state rooms contain a museum outlining the social and industrial history of the area as well as collections of natural history items, fine art and archaeology. There is the **Ynsfach Iron Heritage Centre** based at the old ironworks building which now houses an exhibition which using maps, photographs, models and audio-visual displays illustrates the history of the iron industry in this area. At 4 Chapel Row, Georgetown is the cottage where Dr Joseph Parry, musician and composer was born. Here there is an exhibition devoted to his works and also one devoted to the social and industrial history of 19th-century Merthyr.

On the Cyrfarthfa industrial estate there is also a factory shop belonging to **Bairdwear** which manufactures lingerie for one of the best-known high street chain stores. The factory shops sell seconds and over-makes at as little as one-third of their normal retail price. Stock includes designer wraps, waist slips, full slips, camisoles, bras, French knickers, crop tops and designer nightwear in a wide choice of colours, fabrics and sizes.

Gossard, another leading manufacturer of lingerie, also has a factory shop not too far away at Pontllanfraith which can be reached by travelling south down the A4054 and then east for about six miles on the A472. This factory shop sells seconds and discontinued ranges of Gossard underwear including bras, briefs, suspender belts and bodies, but no nightwear or long-line slips at discounted prices. Most of the stock is last year's trade catalogue styles at discounts of between 25%-75%.

From Pontllanfraith you may wish to finish off your tour by travelling a few miles south down the A469 to **Caerphilly.** There the imposing 13th century castle with its famous leaning tower is the largest in Wales and is surrounded by an intricate system of water defences.

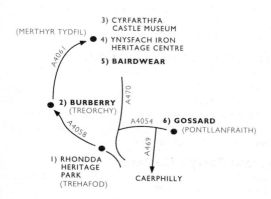

FACTFILE

1) Rhondda Heritage Park
LEWIS MERTHYR, COED CAE RD, TREHAFOD, MID-GLAMORGAN
TEL: 01443 682036
Open: All year daily 10am - 6pm closed Monday from October to
Easter. Last admission 4.30pm. Closed 25th and 26th December.
Admission: £4.95 (Concessions £4.25) family ticket £16.

2) Burberry Factory Shop
YNYSWEN ROAD, TREORCHY, RHONDDA, MID GLAMORGAN
CF42 6EF
TEL: 01443 772020
Open: 9am - 4pm Monday - Thursday, 9am - 2pm Friday, 9am -
1.30pm Saturday

3) Cyfarthfa Castle Museum & Art Gallery
BRECON ROAD, MERTHYR TYDFIL, MID-GLAMORGAN SF47 8RE
TEL: 01865 723112
Open: All year, April - October, Monday - Friday 10am - 6pm,
Saturday and Sunday 12 noon - 6pm. October - March, Monday -
Friday, 10am -5pm, Saturday and Sunday 12noon - 5pm
(Last admission 30 mins before close)
Admission: 90p (children and OAPs 50p)

4) Ynysfach Iron Heritage Centre,
YNYSFACH RD (OFF A470), MERTHYR TYDFIL, MID-GLAMORGAN
TEL: 01865 721858
Open: March - October, Monday - Friday10am - 5pm, Saturday,
Sunday and Bank Holidays 2pm - 5pm. November - February,
Monday - Friday 10am - 5pm (closed weekends and Christmas)
Admission: £1.15 (Concessions 70p)

5) Joseph Parry's Cottage
4 CHAPEL ROW, GEORGETOWN (OFF A470), MID-GLAMORGAN
TEL: 01685 383704/721858
Open: Easter - October, Monday - Friday, 2pm - 5pm, Saturday,
Sunday and Bank Holidays 2pm - 5pm.
Admission: 60p (concessions 50p)

6) Bairdwear Factory Shop
Unit 2, Cyfartha Industrial Estate, Merthyr Tydfil,
Mid Glamorgan, CF47 8PE
Tel: 01685 383837
Open 10am - 4.30pm Monday - Saturday

7) Gossard Factory Shop
Penmaen Road, Pontllanfraith, Blackwood, Gwent,
NT2P 2DL
Tel: 01495 228171
Open 9.30am - 5.30pm Monday - Saturday

8) Caerphilly Castle
Caerphilly, Mid-Glamorgan
Tel: 01222 883143
Open: All year, late October - late March, Monday - Saturday,
9.30am - 4pm, Sunday 11am - 4pm, late March - late Oct daily
9.30-6.30.(Closed 24-26 Dec & 1 Jan).
Admission: £2.20 (children, students and OAPs £1.70,
family ticket (2 adults and up to 3 children under 16 years) £6)

Tour 2
Carreg Cennen, Ammanford, Swansea and the Aberdulais Falls

Carreg Cennan Castle can lay good claim to being the most spectacularly sited fortress in the whole of the Bristish Isles. Perched 330 ft up on a limestone crag from which there are splendid views of the surrounding hill country it has been a stronghold for many centuries being re-built in the late 13th. For those who like atmosphere a wander around this site is a rare experience whereas others may find diversion at the neighbouring farm's rare breeds centre.

From here a journey of about six miles south on the A483 will take you to Ammanford where the urge to shop advantageously may be indulged at the **Alan Paine Knitwear Factory Shop** located at New Rd. The factory shop is actually a small room in the front of the factory itself selling knitwear manufactured in the factory. Most of the knitwear is for men, but women are as likely to buy the round neck sweaters and cardigans. The smallest size they make is a 38" chest. Choose from lambswool, cotton, camel hair, cashmere, merino and merino and silk mix. The company sells to the top shops in London, although most of their stock is made for export.

Heading south on the A483 and M4 will then take you to Swansea. Exit at junction 47 on the A483 and two further miles south will bring you to Fforestfach where on the Industrial Estate is **IJ Dewhirsts Factory Shop.** This contains a wide range of children's, men's and women's clothes including dresses, blouses, trousers, skirts and jackets and much much more.

Head then for the Swansea docks area where in the **Maritime Quarter,** on Victoria Rd, you will find the museum which provides a fund of exciting information and exhibits connected with local history, archaeology and pottery. Close by is found the **Maritime and Industrial Museum** with its selection of floating boats to explore and its exhibits connected with Swansea's commercial and industrial role.

Also on this site is the **Abbey Woollen Mill.** The mill sells pure wool blankets and shawls which have been made on the premises from raw fleeces as well as knitting wool packs, wraps and scarves, all at between 30% and 50% cheaper than the same items in the high street. Every batch is unique and unrepeatable.

Our final stop close to the M4 east of Swansea on the outskirts of Neath is the famous **Aberdulais Falls** at the site of which, now owned by the National Trust, stands a modern hydro-electric plant. The Turbine House at the plant provides visitor access to the top of the falls, a view of the fish pass and various displays.

● (TRAPP)
1) CARREG CENNAN CASTLE
2) ALAN PAINE KNITWEAR FACTORY SHOP
(AMMANFORD)
3) DEWHIRST'S FACTORY SHOP
(FFORESTFACH)
7) ABERDULAIS FALLS
SWANSEA
4/5) MARITIME QUARTER
6) ABBEY WOOLLEN MILL

FACTFILE

1) Carreg Cennan Castle
NR TRAPP, CAR
TEL: 01558 822291
Open: All year from dawn until dusk. Admission: £2.20 (£1.70 for children, OAPs and students) family ticket £6

2) Alan Paine Knitwear Ltd Factory Shop
NEW ROAD INDUSTRIAL ESTATE, AMMANFORD, DYFED, SA18 3ET
TEL: 01269 592316
Open 9am - 4pm Monday - Saturday.

3) Dewhirst Factory Shop
UNIT 22, THE KINGSWAY, FFORESTFACH INDUSTRIAL ESTATE, FFORESTFACH, SWANSEA, WEST GLAMORGAN
TEL: 01792 584621
Open 9am - 5.30pm Monday - Friday, 9am - 5pm Saturday, 10.30am - 4.30pm Sunday

4) Swansea Museum
VICTORIA RD, MARITIME QUARTER, SWANSEA
TEL: 01792 653763
Open: All year round, open Bank Holiday Mondays, Tuesday to Sunday 10am - 5.10pm last entry 4.45pm, closed 25th & 26th December and 1st January. Admission: free

5) Swansea Maritime and Industrial Museum
MUSEUM SQUARE, SWANSEA
TEL: 01792 650351
Open: All year round, Tuesday - Sunday 10.30am - 5.30pm. Last admission 5.00pm. Closed Mondays, 25th , 26th December and 1st January. Admission: free

6) The Abbey Woollen Mill
MARITIME AND INDUSTRIAL MUSEUM, MARITIME QUARTER, SWANSEA, SA1 1SN
TEL: 01792 650351
Open 10am - 5pm Tuesday - Sunday.

7) Aberdulais Falls

ABERDULAIS, NEAR NEATH, WEST GLAMORGAN

TEL: 01639 636674

Open:1st April - 3rd Nov, Monday - Friday 10am - 5pm, Saturday, Sunday and Bank Holidays 11am - 6pm, last entry 30 minutes before closing time. Admission: £2.80, Children £1.40, 1 child under 16 years admitted free with every paying adult. School groups with a minimum of 15 per party £1.10 each, groups of 15 people or more £2.20 each, National Trust members free.

TOUR 3
Trefriw, Conwy, St Asaph and Wrexham

Situated in the beautiful valley of the River Conwy and utilising the rushing waters of a tributary of that river as it dashes headlong for the sea is the **Trefriw Woollen Mill.** The large factory shop attached to the mill sells products manufactured on the premises such as traditional Welsh tapestry bedspreads, from £70 (single bed); travel rugs, £17.50; mohair rugs, £36.95; tweed coats £70; wool, £24.50 a kilo; tweed fabrics from £11.95; tapestries and tweed coats, mohair coats, tweed sports jackets, skirts, ladies coats, ruanas and knitting wool.

A beautiful 10 mile drive north along the B5106 brings you to **Conwy** where the castle built between 1283 and 1289 by Edward I to help subdue the unruly Welsh is a truly magnificent site.and a masterpiece of medieval military architecture. Perhaps the best view to be had of it is from the east bank of the river estuary where the mountains of Snowdonia form provide a superb scenic backcloth. There is much of interest inside the castle as well of which regular tours are available

The next shopping stop is St Asaph about 20 miles east along the A55 where the **Tweedmill Factory Shopping Centre** is located at Llanerch Park. This has a wide range of ladies clothes, both designer and top end of the high street, and childrenswear, as well as handbags, scarves, blankets and ties. There are ladies jackets from Racing Green, Lakeland and a variety of good quality high street fashion stores. For example, Lakeland trousers at £29.95, and leather jackets from £79, all of which represent discounts of up to 60%. Labels on sale include Feminella, Jersey Masters, Pierre Cardin, Double Two and Barry Sherrrard as well as high street names such as Principles.

About two miles before St Asaph on the A55 you will have passed signs for Bodelwyddan Castle. If you like Victorian style and paintings this country house is well worth visiting. There are over 200 Victorian portraits on loan there from the National Portrait Gallery and the 19th century interiors of the house provide the perfect setting for these. John Singer-Sargent and Holman Hunt are among the painters exhibited and in addition to these paintings there is Victorian furniture from the V&A and sculptures from the Royal Academy

To round off this tour head east from St Asaph along the A55 and then take the A483 to Wrexham where there are two shops to visit. There at Holt Rd, albeit with rather limited opening hours, is **Velmore Fashions** where you can buy overmakes of skirts, jackets and trousers originally made for the most famous high street name at very cheap prices. Also at Rhosddu Rd is **Scoops** which is part of a chain of shops used by Grattan, the mail order company to clear their overstocks. There is a selection of items from those featured in the catalogue, which can consist of anything from children's clothes and toys to bedding, electrical equipment and nursery accessories. Each shop sells a slightly different range, so always ring first to check they stock what you want. All items are discounted by between 30% and 50%.

If you've not used up all your time shopping you may want to visit **Erddig House** just south of Wrexham off the A525. The house is full of interesting utensils, tools and memorabilia which give a good picture of its occupants's lives. Built in 1680, the original furnishings are still there and most of the estate outbuildings have been restored. The garden is also very much like the 18th century original.

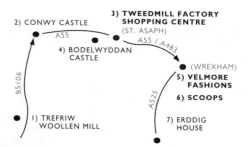

FACTFILE

1) Trefriw Woollen Mill Shop

TREFRIW, NR. GWYNEDD LL27 ONQ

TEL: 01492 640462

Open 9am - 5pm Monday - Friday, 10am - 5pm Saturday during winter months; 9am - 5.30pm Monday - Friday, 10am - 5pm Saturday during summer months

2) Conwy Castle

CONWY, GWYNEDD. TEL: 01492 592358

Open: all year, late October - late March, Monday - Saturday 9.30am - 4pm, Sunday 11am - 4pm, late March - late October daily 9.30-6.30 (closed 24th, 25th, 26th December and 1st January Admission: £3 (£2 children and OAPs) family ticket, 2 adults and up to 3 children £8.

3) Tweedmill Factory Shopping

LLANNERCH PARK, ST ASAPH, CLYWD

TEL: 01745 730072

Open 10am - 6pm seven days a week.

4) Bodelwyddan Castle

BODELWYDDAN, NR ST ASAPH, CLWYD

TEL: 01745 584060

Open: all year daily except Fridays from Easter - October 10am - 5pm, daily July and August 10am - 5pm, November - March open daily except Mondays and Fridays 11am - 4pm last entry 1 hour before closing. Admission: £4.00 (children and students £2.50, OAPs £3.50)

5) Velmore Fashions

1-2 JAEGER HOUSE, 141 HOLT ROAD, WREXHAM, CLWYD, LL13 9DY

TEL: 01978 363456

Open 10.30am - 3pm Monday, Wednesday, Friday.

6) Scoops
7-9 RHOSDDU ROAD, WREXHAM, CLWYD LL11 1AR
TEL: 01978 266450
Open 9am - 5.30pm Monday - Saturday.

7) Errdig
NR WREXHAM (OFF THE A525)
TEL: 01978 355314
Open: 1st April - 2nd October daily except Thursday and Friday,
Garden 11am - 6pm, House 12 noon - 5pm, last admission 4pm.
Admission: £5.20 (children £2.60,
family ticket 2 adults 2 children £8.50)

THE WEST MIDLANDS

This is an area well known for its large sprawling industrial conurbations – Birmingham with its surrounding satellite towns and, of course, the 'Black Country' with its potteries – but there are also large tracts of unspoilt countryside with attractive market towns and villages and, even in the centre of these urban sprawls, there are buildings and sites with the visual impact and historical resonance to excite any visitor. And, cheek by jowl with all of them, are to be found factory and discount outlets offering some very special goods at very special prices.

TOUR 1
Worcester, the Malverns and the Vale of Evesham

The sight of Worcester cathedral viewed from the meadows to the south of the River Severn is one of the classic scenes of rural England. Worcester is a busy county town but in the late 20th century it has still not lost its old world charm. A boating trip along the Severn is always enjoyable here and visiting the much celebrated cathedral is an essential ingredient of any tour. Work began on the cathedral in 1084 and continued for many years – its architecture being a harmonious blend of many different styles. The cathedral contains the tomb of King John, one of England's less revered monarchs, as well as that of Prince Arthur, Henry Vlll's elder brother and the first husband of Catherine of Aragon.

When the urge to shop takes you it's comforting to know that from the cathedral it's very little distance to the **Royal Worcester shop** on Severn Street. There you can purchase infinitesimally flawed porcelain and china seconds at 25% less than "perfect" prices. The shop also sells Royal Brierley, Dartington, Caithness and Stuart Crystal as well as Arthur Price cutlery. There is a vast range with special offers throughout the year on anything from crystal decanters and bowls to figurines, cookware and dinner sets. You need not take it away on the spot either as shipping arrangements can be organised to anywhere in the world.

Another bargain outlet in Worcester that is well worth a visit is **G R Pratley & Sons,** a family business which specialises in bone china and earthenware, selling famous designer names at 15% lower than normal retail prices. Manufacturers include Wedgwood, Royal Worcester and Spode and individual pieces as well as sets can be bought. They also stock reproduction furniture, good quality country style furniture, rugs and chinese carpets which start at £70.

A six-mile drive south west of Worcester on the A449 will then take you into the **Malvern Hills** from where there are marvellous views westward to the Black Mountains and Brecon Beacons of Wales and eastward over the Vale of Evesham. The town of Great Malvern on its attractive terraced hillside site posseses the magnificent Norman Priory Chuch of SS Mary and Michael built only 20 years after the conquest in 1086.

Any lady with a taste for designer clothes at bargain prices should then follow on with a visit to **The Studio** at 11 Abbey Rd. Here are stocked the finest designer clothes from the continent at discounts of 50%. The company's team of buyers search out and secure considerable discounts on top European name ranges which include both this season's stock and next. The names are well-known but they cannot be divulged here – suffice it to say that they are excellent labels. All stock is perfect, and the vast range covers from casual wear to special occasion outfits.

From Great Malvern you may want to carry on west to Little Malvern where Edward Elgar lies buried in the yard of the Roman Catholic church. Swinging east from here about 15 miles along the A4104 will take you to **Pershore a** delightful Georgian town situated on the north bank of the Avon. Apart from the delights of its architecture, its hotels and inns, Pershore High Street also boasts **The Curtain Rack.** This shop contains three large showrooms, including a Designer Showroom, packed with full-length designer curtains, many from London, for about one third of the original cost value. The enormous selection caters for all budgets from low cost curtains ideal for rented accommodation through to magnificent curtains fit for a palace. There is also a wide selection of fabrics at competitive prices, a made-to-measure service and customers can take curtains home on approval.

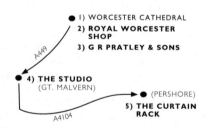

FACTFILE

1) Worcester Cathedral
WORCESTER, WORCESTERSHIRE
TEL: 01905 28854
Open daily 7.30am to 6.00pm. Tower open in summer on Saturdays from 11.30am. No admission charge

2) Royal Worcester
SEVERN ST, WORCESTER, WR1 2NE
TEL: 01905 23221
Open 9am - 5.30pm Monday - Saturday

3) G R Pratley & Sons
THE SHAMBLES, WORCESTER, WR1 2RG
TEL: 01905 22678
Open 9am - 5.30pm Monday - Saturday, closes at 1pm on Thursdays

4) Studio
11 ABBEY RD, GREAT MALVERN, WORCESTERSHIRE WR14 3ES
TEL: 01684 576253
Open: 9am - 5.30 pm Monday - Saturday

5) The Curtain Rack
25 HIGH ST, PERSHORE, WORCESTERSHIRE, WR10 1AA
TEL: 01386 556105
Open 10am -4.30pm Monday - Friday, 9.30am - 5.30 pm Saturday

TOUR 2
Tamworth, Lichfield and Stafford

There are a number of reasons to recommend a visit to Tamworth. Foremost among the sights is a fine and ancient castle which was built by the Normans but has been considerably added to since. There is a splendid timber - roofed Tudor banqueting hall and Jacobean oak-panelled state dining room and the long gallery has now been made into a fascinating museum housing exhibits from the castle's past. A lot of the rooms also have scenes depicting the lives of the castle's former occupants. The **town hall,** built in 1701 by Thomas Guy (the founder of Guy's Hospital in London) is one of the most attractive in the country constructed as it is in mellow red brick and possessing large Jacobean windows. The parish church of **St Editha** is also rather unusual in design and certainly worth a visit.

Tamworth's two factory shops should be next on your list. At 42 Church St is the **Jaeger factory shop.** There you will find classic tailoring at old-fashioned prices. This is a large shop which deals mainly in separates and casual wear from last year's stock. For example, skirts, £39, originally £89; jackets, £65, originally £289. Most of the merchandise is last season's or earlier stock and some seconds. There is also an **Alexon Sale Shop** at 34 George St where you can obtain Alexon, Eastex and Dash from last season at 40% less than the original price; during sale time in January and June, the reductions are as much as 70%. Stock includes separates, skirts, jackets, blouses, and leisurewear; there is no underwear or night clothes.

It is about 6 miles up the A51 from Tamworth to **Lichfield**. Here there is situated one of England's smaller **cathedrals** built in red sandstone and begun in the 1190s. One of its priceless possessions are the Herckenrode windows in the Lady Chapel which originally belonged to a Cistercian abbey in Belgium.

Among Lichfield's famous sons are Elias Ashmole whose collection of antiquities formed the basis of the Ashmolean Museum in Oxford, and Dr Samuel Johnson, the 18th century lexicographer and writer. Johnson's birthplace on the corner of Breadmarket St is now a museum of Johnsonian relics and his statue sits at one end of the market square.

On the discount shopping tour Lichfield also has something to offer, namely the **Arthur Price of England Factory shop.** This factory shop sells seconds, discontinued lines and shop-soiled samples of silver-plated and stainless steel cutlery. There are sets as well as loose items on sale at half price or less. Also on sale is giftware consisting of candelabras, cruet sets, tea services, tankards and trays, most at half price. There are usually two sales a year - in October and March - when there is an extra 20%-25% off.

Another rather longer trip of about 12 miles up the A51 and A513 will then take you to **Shugborough** a magnificent 18th century mansion and the seat of the Anson family, Earls of Lichfield. It posesses a Grade 1 listed historic garden with a unique collection of neo-classical monuments and a Georgian farmhouse with an agricultural museum, working corn mill and rare breeds centre.

From Shugborough a five mile journey up the A513 will take you into Stafford where your trip can be rounded off with a visit to the **Schott Zwiesel factory shop** at the Astonfields industrial estate. Europe's largest manufacturer of blown crystal glassware, Schott Zwiesel has been established for more than 100 years. They make fine cut crystal stemware, plain crystal stemware, crystal giftware and blown decorative crystal. The factory shop sells a variety of glassware including stemware, glass bowls, heat resistant glass, vases, rosebowls, sets of handmade crystal, boxed presentation sets with matching decanters, tankards and fruit bowls.

8) SCHOTT ZWIESEL
FACTORY SHOP
(STAFFORD)

A513

7) SHUGBOROUGH
ESTATE

(LICHFIELD)

(TAMWORTH)

A51

A51

4) LICHFIELD CATHEDRAL

5) SAMUEL JOHNSON
BIRTHPLACE MUSEUM

6) **ARTHUR PRICE OF ENGLAND
FACTORY SHOP**

1) TAMWORTH CASTLE

2) **JAEGER FACTORY SHOP**

3) **ALEXON SALE SHOP**

FACTFILE

1) Tamworth Castle
THE HOLLOWAY, TAMWORTH, STAFFS.
TEL: 01827 635653
Open: all year Monday to Saturday 10am - 5.30pm, Sunday
2pm - 5.30pm. Admission: £3.20. OAPs £1.60 Family £8.00

2) Jaeger Factory Shop
42 CHURCH STREET, TAMWORTH, STAFFORDSHIRE B79 7DE
TEL: 01827 52828
Open: 9.30am - 5.30pm Monday - Saturday

3) Alexon Sale Shop
34 GEORGE STREET, TAMWORTH, STAFFORDSHIRE
TEL: 01827 310041
Open: 9am - 5.30pm Monday - Saturday

4) Lichfield Cathedral
THE CLOSE, LICHFIELD, STAFFORDSHIRE.
TEL: 01543 256120
Open: 7.45am - 6.15pm daily, Sundays 7.45am - 4.30pm during
winter, 7.45am - 8pm during summer. Admission: free, you can make
a donation if you so wish

5) Samuel Johnson Birthplace Museum

BREADMARKET STREET, LICHFIELD, STAFFORDSHIRE WS13 6LG
TEL: 01543 264972
Open: daily 10am - 5pm (closed Christmas & New Year)
Admission £1.20 (children & OAPs 70p), family ticket (2 adults and
up to 4 children) £3.20. Joint ticket combining above and Lichfield
Heritage Centre £2.20 (children and OAPs £1.20)

6) Arthur Price of England Factory Shop

BRITANNIA WAY, BRITTANIA ENTERPRISE PARK, LICHFIELD,
STAFFORDSHIRE WS14 9UY
TEL: 01543 257775
Open: 9am - 5pm Monday - Friday, 9am - 1pm Saturday

7) Shugborough Estate

MILFORD, NR STAFFORD, STAFFORDSHIRE ST17 0XB
TEL: 01889 881388
Open: Saturday 23rd March - Sunday 29th September every day
11am - 5pm. Booked parties from 10.30am. Admission £3.50
(children, OAPs and groups £2.50). All - in tickets available.
Site admission fee to parkland, gardens and picnic area £1.50.

8) Schott Zwiesel Factory Shop

DRUMMOND ROAD, ASTONFIELDS INDUSTRIAL ESTATE, STAFFORD
STAFFORDSHIRE ST16 3EL
TEL: 01785 223166
Open: 10am - 4.30pm Monday - Friday, 10am - 3pm Saturday.

TOUR 3
Stoke-On-Trent and the Potteries

Anyone interested in industrial and social history will want to visit
Stoke-On-Trent. Until the Industrial Revolution Stoke was a mere
village around a church. By 1910 it had grown to such a degree that it
was combined with the five surrounding towns: Tunstall, Burslem,
Hanley, Longton and Fenton to form a new Stoke-On-Trent. The
impetus for this stunning growth had come from the pottery industry
and the development from the late 18th century onwards of such names
as Wedgwood, Spode, Minton and Doulton.

A visit to the **City Museum and Art Gallery** on Bethesda St is very helpful to an understanding of the history of the Potteries and it includes an amazing display of ceramics containing more than 500 pieces mainly sourced from the area. Other displays outline the social, natural and archaeological history of the area.

Wedgwood is the name most often heard in connection with the history of the Potteries and a visit to the Wedgwood visitor centre in Barlaston helps explain why. A video outlines the history of Wedgwood pottery and demonstrates the techniques employed and the complex also includes an art gallery with works by leading English painters of the 18th century such as Stubbs, Reynolds and Romney.

Of course all the leading potteries have their factory shops offering the chance to buy beautiful china at reduced prices and the details of where to go and when are all given in the Factfile section.

Making your own way by car around all the different factory shops can be frustrating, as they are sited in different parts of the city. Make for the station and take a bus tour round the potteries and save yourself stress.

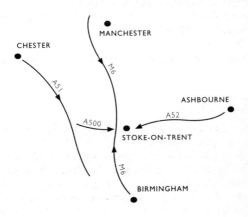

FACTFILE

1) City Museum and Art Gallery

BETHESDA STREET, HANLEY, STOKE-ON-TRENT, STAFFORDSHIRE
ST1 3DW
TEL: 01782 202173
Open: Monday - Saturday 10am - 5, Sun 2- 5 (closed Christmas and
New Year). Admssion: Free

2) Wedgwood Visitor Centre

BARLASTON, STOKE-ON-TRENT, STAFFORDSHIRE ST12 9ES
TEL: 01782 204141 & 204218.
Open: Monday - Friday 9am - 5pm (including Bank Holidays),
Saturday 10am - 5pm, Sunday 10am - 4pm. Closed Christmas and
New Year Holidays.

3) Aynsley China Factory Shop

SUTHERLAND ROAD, LONGTON, STOKE-ON-TRENT,
STAFFORDSHIRE ST3 1HS
TEL: 01782 593536
Open 9am - 5.30pm Monday - Saturday, 10am - 4pm Sunday.
Also at:
UNIT N, LEWIS'S ARCADE, POTTERIES SHOPPING CENTRE, HANLEY,
STOKE-ON-TRENT, STAFFORDSHIRE ST1 1PS
TEL: 01782 204108.
Open 9am - 5.30pm Monday - Saturday

4) Blakeney Art Pottery

WOLFE STREET, STOKE-ON-TRENT, STAFFORDSHIRE ST4 4DA
TEL: 01782 847244.
Open: 9am - 4.30 pm Monday - Thursday, 9am - 3.30pm Friday

5) Moorland Pottery

CHELSEA WORKS, 72A MOORLAND ROAD, BURSLEM,
STOKE-ON-TRENT, STAFFORDSHIRE ST6 1DY
TEL: 01782 834631.
Open: 9am - 5pm Monday - Friday, 10am - 4pm Saturday

6) Portmeirion

Silvan Works, Normacott Road, Longton,
Stoke-On-Trent, Staffs. ST3 1PW
TEL: 01782 326412.
Open 9.30am - 5pm Monday - Friday, 9.30am - 3pm Saturday
Also at: 25 George Street, Newcastle-Under-Lyme,
Staffordshire
TEL: 01782 615192.
Open 9.30am - 5.30pm Monday - Friday, 9.30am - 4pm Saturday
Also at: London Road, Stoke, Staffordshire
TEL: 01782 411756
Open 9.15am - 5.15 Mon - Friday 9.15am - 3.30 pm Saturday

7) Price & Kensington Potteries Ltd.

Trubshaw Cross, Longport, Stoke-On-Trent, Staffordshire
ST6 4LR
TEL: 01782 838631
Open 9.45am - 5pm Monday - Saturday

8) Royal Doulton Factory Shop

Minton House, London Road, Stoke-On-Trent,
Staffordshire ST4 7QD
TEL: 01782 292121
Open: 9am - 5.30 pm Monday - Saturday The above sells Minton
and a small selection of Royal Doulton. Other factory shops at:

9) Leek

New Road, Baddeley Green
sells seonds tableware and best quality giftware.
TEL: 01782 291700

Nile Street, Burslem
sells best quality showroom and there is also a museum here.
TEL: 01782 292451

Victoria Road, Fenton
sells Royal Albert, Royal Doulton seconds.
TEL: 01782 291869

All the above are within a five mile radius.

10) Royal Grafton China Factory Shop
MARLBOROUGH ROAD, LONGTON, STOKE-ON-TRENT,
STAFFORDSHIRE ST3 1ED
TEL: 01782 599667
Open: 9am - 4.30pm Monday - Friday, 9am - 3pm Saturday

11) Salisbury China
45 UTTOXETER ROAD, LONGTON, STOKE-ON-TRENT,
STAFFORDSHIRE ST3 1NY
TEL: 01782 333466
Open: 10.30am - 4pm Monday - Saturday

12) Spode
CHURCH STREET, STOKE-ON-TRENT, STAFFORDSHIRE ST4 1BX
TEL: 01782 744011
Open: 9am - 5pm Monday - Saturday, 10am - 4pm Sunday

13) Wedgwood Group Factory Shop
KING STREET, FENTON, STOKE-ON-TRENT, STAFFORDSHIRE
ST4 3DQ
TEL: 01782 316161.
Open: 9am - 5pm Monday - Saturday and Bank Holidays
10am - 4pm Sunday

EAST ANGLIA AND THE EAST MIDLANDS

This geographical grouping covers a wide range of contrasting countryside as we go from the flat, expansive landscape and big skies of Norfolk and Lincolnshire, where the horizon is often dotted with church steeples, to the hills and mills of Derbyshire. There our final journey takes us to Ashbourne, the gateway to Dovedale, where we flirt with the drama of the Pennine peaks. As an area for factory and discount shopping East Anglia – Norfolk, Suffolk, Cambridgeshire and the Wash – has generally rather less to offer than other more industrialised parts of the the British Isles. However, there are still some excellent places to visit, as there are in the East Midlands, where there is decidedly more from which to choose.

TOUR 1
Norwich, Aylsham, Holt and Cromer

Our tour starts in the centre of the ancient medieval city of Norwich at the **Castle Museum** which is housed in the 12th century Norman keep. The museum contains a fascinating display of archaeology, natural history and art with particular emphasis on the Norwich School of painters represented by such fine exponents as John Crome and John Sell Cotman. It also houses silver and Lowestoft porcelain and there are also guide tours of the Castle.

Of course, there are lots of other sites to take in in Norwich if you have the time, such as the superb Norman cathedral and many other impressive churches such as St Peter Mancroft and the medieval streets around Elm Hill.

Our first port of call on the shopping tour takes us to the **Bally Factory shop** in Hall Rd. This is situated next to the main factory and sells women's and men's footwear, and accessories for women and men such as hosiery, socks, scarves, shoe horns and shoe care products. Also sold are leather handbags, briefcases, suitcovers, holdalls and overnight cases. Most of the merchandise is seconds, substandard, ends of line or ex-sale stock and is priced from £5-£200, which is usually at least one-third off the recommended retail price. There is also a coffee shop which serves morning coffee, light lunches and afternoon teas, a children's play area, toilet facilities, free parking and disabled facilities. Within the factory shop, there is also a full price department which sells all the current styles. A small "museum" is incorporated within the shop showing the history of shoe-making since the Roman times and the history of Bally, with examples of shoes on display. Coach parties are welcome by prior arrangement. Factory tours are not available.

From here you should head north out of Norwich up the A140 to Aylsham. Here there is another factory shop which is well worth trying if you are looking for bathroom or kitchen equipment. The **Aylsham Bath & Door Company** has bathroom equipment, kitchen displays, bedroom fittings, all at reduced prices of at least 20%- 25% less than normal retail prices. Top brands such as Dalton, Ideal Standard, Armitage, Shires and Shanks are some of the 70 bathrooms displayed here; and there are 30 display kitchens with appliances by Neff, Philips, Whirlpool and Zanussi.

Carrying on north out of Aylsham on the B1354 you will very shortly pick up signs for **Blickling Hall.** This Jacobean house is one of the country's greatest inheritances. Much earlier buildings dating from the time of King Harold once stood here, the property passing on through the hands of various families including the Boleyns. The present house was built between 1616 and 1627 for Sir Henry Hobart. The exterior and interior are quite splendid. There is a great carved staircase, a magnificent ante-room, drawing room and dining room and, perhaps best of all, the gallery with its decorative plaster ceiling. The many paintings include a Canaletto and the grounds and gardens are extensive.

Carrying on north up the B1354 and B1149 will bring you to **Holt,** a pleasant town and the site of the famous Gresham's school founded in 1555 by Sir Thomas Gresham. The Hempstead Rd Industrial Estate in Holt is the site of **Ashford Hall Ltd** whose factory shop sells overstocks of preserves, pickles, jams, biscuits and salts which they make for well known stores and under their own label. They also make gift baskets, food hampers and sell cookshop items and aromatic herbs.

A journey of about 10 miles east on the A148 will then bring you to the delightful seaside resort of **Cromer.** The cottages of the original fishing village are grouped picturesquely on top of the cliffs. Housed in five of these fishermen's cottages in Tucker St is the **Cromer Museum.** Here, in this charming setting, there are exhibits and pictures of Victorian Cromer and collections illustrating local natural history, geology, social history and archaeology. There are good sandy beaches at Cromer too and cliff top walks with fine views may be taken North and South of the town.

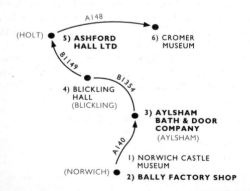

FACTFILE

1) Norwich Castle Museum

CASTLE MEADOW, NORWICH, NORFOLK
TEL: 01603 223624
Open: All year, Monday - Saturday 10am - 5pm, Sunday 2pm - 5pm
(closed Good Friday, 24th, 25th, 26th December and 1st January).
Admission: £2.20 (children £1, OAPs £1.50) July and August prices:
£3 (children, £2, OAPs £1.40)

2) Bally Factory Shop

HALL RD, NORWICH, NORFOLK, NR4 6DP
TEL: 01603 760590
Open: 9.30am - 5.30pm Monday - Fri,day 9am - 5.30pm Saturday
and Bank Holidays 10am - 4pm

3) Aylsham Bath & Door

BURGH RD, AYLSHAM, NORFOLK. NR11 6AR
TEL: 01263 735396
Open: 8.30am - 5pm Monday - Friday, 9am - 5pm Saturday,
10 am - 4pm Sunday.

4) Blickling Hall

BLICKLING, NR AYLSHAM, NORFOLK
TEL: 01263 733084
Open: 23rd March - 3rd November, Hall 12.30pm - 4.30, Gardens,
restaurant shop and plant centre 10.30am - 5.30pm. In July and
August hall and gardens are open every day. Hall closed Mondays and
Thursdays except Bank Holiday Mondays. Admission: £5.50 (children
£2.50) Tuesday, Wednesday, Friday and Saturday for Hall and gardens.
£6.50 (children £2.75) for Sundays and Bank Holiday Mondays.
Gardens only £3.20 (children £1.60) Tuesday, Wednesday, Friday
Saturday. £3.50 (children £1.75) Sunday and Bank Holiday Mondays.
Family ticket, 2 adults plus 2 children for hall and gardens £13 any day.
Garden only, any day, £7.

5) Ashford Hall Ltd Factory Shop

UNIT 4A, HEMPSTEAD ROAD, INDUSTRIAL ESTATE, HOLT,
NORFOLK NR25 6EC
TEL: 01263 711447
Open: 9am - 5pm Monday - Friday, 9am - 5pm Saturday, and special
Sundays

6) Cromer Museum

EAST COTTAGES, TUCKER STREET, CROMER, NORFOLK
NR27 9HB
TEL: 01263 513543
Open: All year, Monday - Saturday 10am - 5pm, Sunday 2pm - 5pm.
(closed Monday 1pm - 2pm and Good Friday, 24th, 25th, 26th
December and January 1st). Admission: £1 (children 50p, OAPs,
students 60p)

TOUR 2
Riddings, Denby, Derby, Kedleston Hall and Ashbourne

This tour starts at Riddings in Derbyshire where the **Charnos factory shop** is situated at the Amber Business Centre, Greenhill Lane. Here about 25% of the shop is given over to discontinued perfects of the famous Charnos lingerie at discounts of 25%-50%. Current ladies lingerie is discounted by 25%, discontinued lingerie by 50%. The rest of the shop stocks wool, acrylic and cotton knitwear for women and men at factory shop prices, and bought-in bedding, towelling and babywear, cards and giftwrap at very competitive prices. Some stock is grade B quality.

From here head west to Swanwick and then south down the B6179 to Denby where there is the **Denby Pottery Visitors Centre.** Here the potter's craft is illustrated with guided factory tours in which you can witness throwing, turning, glazing and decorating and the on-site museum outlines the history of Denby Pottery. There is also a factory shop selling famous Denby pottery perfects and seconds in tableware, cookware, mugs, informal dining sets, cutlery, pans, lamps and vases as well as seconds in Dartington Crystal. Seconds are sold at 25% less than the normal retail price, with even greater discounts at sale times. There are also bargain baskets with pottery which costs up to 75% less than its original price. Special sales are held twice a year in January and June.

If you're interested in purchasing more brand name pottery you can then take the A38 south to Derby where at 194 Osmaston Rd the **Royal Crown Derby factory shop** is sited. One third of the stock in this small shop is made up of seconds of bone china at discount prices of about one third off the normal retail price. This includes giftware, tableware and paperweights. Tours can be booked and cream teas arranged.

A short journey west along the A52 is all it then needs to reach **Kedleston Hall** which many consider to be the finest Robert Adam house of them all. Not that it was all built by Adam - James Paine built the impressive north front with its triumphal arch and giant columns – but Adam designed the south front and much of the interior. The marble hall containing 20 giant alabaster columns, an Italian marble floor, alcoves with statues and beautifully painted panels must be one of the most splendid rooms in Europe. The site has been the home of the Curzons for over 8 centuries and it is due to Lord Curzon, the Victorian Viceroy of India, that there is an Indian Museum containing silver, ivories, ancient weapons and oriental art. The grounds contain a boathouse and bridge both designed by Adam as well as the 13th century Church of All Saints which contains some fascinating Curzon monuments.

Our final stop on this tour takes us a few miles further up the A52 to Ashbourne, the gateway to the Peak district. Here, at Shawcroft, is the **Derwent Crystal factory shop** where you can buy a wide selection of glassware and fancy items at factory shop prices. The glassware comprises full English lead crystal from liqueur glasses to vases and bowls, ringstands and dressing-table novelties. More than 200 different items on sale and a gift wrap service is available.

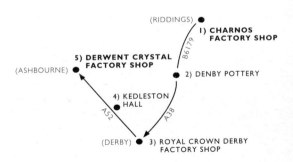

FACTFILE

1) Charnos Factory Shop
AMBER BUSINESS CENTRE, GREENHILL LANE, RIDDINGS,
DERBYSHIRE. DE55 4BR
TEL: 01773 540408
Open: 10am - 4pm Tuesday - Friday, 9.30am - 1pm Saturday

2) Denby Pottery
POTTERY LANE DENBY, DERBYSHIRE DE5 8NX
TEL: 01773 570684 SHOP - 01773 743641
RECEPTION (NOT AVAILABLE WEEKENDS)
Open 9am - 5pm Monday - Saturday, 10am - 5pm Sunday.
Factory Tours: Monday -Thursday 10.30am - 1pm, Friday 11am
Admission: factory tours £3.10 (children & OAPs £2.10)

3) Royal Crown Derby Factory Shop
194 OSMASTON RD, DERBY, DERBYSHIRE. DE23 8JZ
TEL: (01332) 712833
Open: 9am - 5.30pm Monday - Friday, 9 am - 4.30pm Saturday,
Sunday 10am - 4pm
Factory Tours: two tours per day 10.30am and 2.45pm, 1.15 on
Fridays. Admission: £3 (children and OAPs £2.75). Party of 30 or
more adults £2.50, 30 or more OAPs £2.25. NB No children under
10 years allowed on factory floor.

4) Kedleston Hall
KEDLESTON, DERBYSHIRE
TEL: 01332 842191
Open: **House:** March - October, Saturday - Wednesday, 1pm -
5.30pm, last admission 5pm (closed Good Friday); Garden: same as
house but open 11am - 6pm
Admission: £4.50 (children £2.20, family ticket £11.20)
Park & Garden only: April - October daily 11am - 6pm,
Admission: £2 (children £1) refundable on purchase of ticket for
house when open.
Open: November - 22nd December Saturday and Sunday
12 noon - 4pm

5) Derwent Crystal

SHAWCROFT, ASHBOURNE, DERBYSHIRE. DE6 1GH

TEL: 01335 345219

Open: 9am - 5pm Monday - Saturday. Factory Tours to see glassblowing 9am - 1.30pm Monday - Friday. Please pre-book for parties of over 10 people or more. Admission: free.

TOUR 3
Grantham, Belton House and Lincoln

This tour starts in Grantham, Lincs., which it would be a shame to visit without at least a quick stop at the great mainly 14th century church of **St Wulframs** whose 281 ft steeple is a landmark for miles around. Of particular interest, along with the beauties of the Lady Chapel, is the north porch and the double vaulted crypt. To the east of the church is the 14th century **Grantham House** which once housed Margaret Tudor, the daughter of Henry VII as she made her way north to marry James IV of Scotland.

A shopping opportunity well worth looking at in Grantham is **M.C. Hitchen & Sons** at 7, The High St. Littlewoods sell off their overstocks in a network of M.C.Hitchen shops. Most of them are in the north of England and offer up to 40% off the catalogue price for clothing and between 50% and 60% off for electrical goods. Stock changes constantly and varies from day to day but can include well-known brand names such as Berlei and Gossard lingerie, Vivienne Westwood, Pamplemousse leisure wear, Nike and Adidas sports shoes, Workers for Freedom, and Timberland and Caterpillar footwear. Stock depends on the size and location of the shop, so larger shops will get the longer discontinued runs and smaller shops over-runs with only a small amount of colour and size variations left.

Before leaving Grantham you should also try **Lincolshire Craft Workshops** at 4 Hollis Rd. They supply leather goods, pine furniture and cold cast bronze to outlets in London, using the very best quality materials. Individual shoppers can visit their workshop in Grantham and buy goods at factory direct prices which usually means discounts of 5%-15%. For example, a Victorian bed, £400; carved bed, £280; Malvern bed, £196; four-poster, £656; farmhouse table, £156, and chairs, from £41 each; double tower CD holder for 80 CDs, £25. The leather goods include a wallet holding eight credit cards, money clips, writing sets, manicure sets. In cold cast bronze are hedgehogs, kingfishers, blue tit key hooks, tawny owl wall motifs in bronze and 3-D fish plaques. (Please phone before visiting as opening times were changing as we went to press.)

From here head north east on the A607 Lincoln Rd where only 3 miles out of the town you will come upon **Belton House.** This is the ancestral home of the Brownlow family that dates from the reign of William & Mary being built in 1689 from designs by Sir Christopher Wren. It is a grand mansion but not overwhelming with splendid furnishings and decorations throughout. It has some superb wood carvings in the Grinling Gibbons style and a fine collection of paintings and tapestries, antique silver and porcelain. The gardens, laid out in the 19th century, include an orangery and an Italian formal garden.

Carrying on northwards up the A607 it is about another 22 miles to **Lincoln.** No visit to this city is complete without stopping at the great Norman **cathedral** which is the third largest in England after St Pauls and York Minster with an area of about 57,000 sq ft. The original cathedral was completed in 1092 but an earthquake caused devastating damage in 1185 resulting in an immense re-building project which began in 1192 under the then Bishop, Hugh of Avalon. This gave rise to the glorious Early English style edifice that we behold today on the crown of Lincoln hill.

With its Norman castle, county and social history museums there is plenty to visit in this city which still retains much of the character and feel of its noble past. There are also a number of interesting shopping opportunities that should not be missed.

Discount Dressing at 45 Steep Hill is a veritable Aladdin's Cave of designer bargains. They sell mostly German, Italian and French designer labels at prices at least 50% and up to 90% below those in normal retail outlets, and all items are brand new and perfect. They have a team of buyers all over Europe who purchase stock directly from the manufacturer, therefore by-passing the importers and wholesalers and, of course, their mark-up. They also buy bankrupt stock in this country. Their agreement with their suppliers means that they are not able to advertise brand names for obvious reasons, but they are all well-known for their top quality and style. So confident is Discount Dressing that you will be unable to find the same item cheaper elsewhere, that they offer to give the outfit to you free of charge should you perform this miracle.

Merchandise includes raincoats, dresses, suits, trousers, blouses, evening wear, special occasion outfits and jackets, in sizes 6-24 and in some cases larger.

Moving on **Lincoln Cloth Market** at 83 Bailgate stocks Liberty, Jane Churchill, Ramm Son & Crocker, Christian Fischbacher and Harlequin wallpaper, and a range of discounted fabric. It also sells dress fabrics, border wallpaper, cottons and silks. There are usually seconds in various fabrics at one third to one half of the original price, and a catalogue of wedding dress fabrics.

Finally, if you're looking for net or printed cotton curtains **The Curtain Factory Shop** at 279 High Street makes net curtains on the premises for well-known high street department stores and sells them at half the price you would pay in the high street. Eighty percent of the stock is net curtaining from basic net to French voiles; 20% is printed cotton curtaining. Nets range from £1 a metre to £8 with fabric from £1.99 a yard to £5.99 a yard and remnants from 50p.

(LINCOLN) ● 4) DISCOUNT DRESSING
5) LINCOLN CLOTH MARKET
A 607
6) THE CURTAIN
FACTORY SHOP

● 3) BELTON HOUSE

1) M. C. HITCHEN AND SONS
(GRANTHAM) ● 2) LINCOLNSHIRE CRAFT WORKSHOP

FACTFILE

1) M C Hitchen & Sons Ltd
7 HIGH STREET, GRANTHAM, LINCOLNSHIRE, NG31 6PN
TEL: 01476 590552
Open: 9.30am - 5.30pm Monday 9am - 5.30pm Tuesday - Saturday

2) Lincolnshire Craft Workshops
UNIT 4 HOLLIS RD, GRANTHAM, LINCOLNSHIRE. NG31 7QH
TEL: 01476 79728
Open: 9.30am - 4.30pm Monday - Friday 8.30 pm - 12 noon Saturday

3) Belton House
BELTON, GRANTHAM, LINCOLNSHIRE
TEL: (01476) 66116
Open: **House:** 1pm - 5.30pm 31st March - 31st October,
Wednesday - Sunday and Bank Holiday Mondays (closed Good Fri);
last admission 5pm. **Grounds:** 11am - 5.30pm open on same days as
house. Admission: £4.50 (children £2.20, family ticket £11.20)

4) Discount Dressing
45 STEEP HILL, LINCOLN. LN2 1LU
TEL: 01522 532239
Open: 10am - 6pm Monday - Saturday and selected Sundays.

5) Lincoln Cloth Market
83 BAILGATE, LINCOLN. LN1 3AR
TEL: 01522 529872
Open: 9.30am - 5.30pm Monday - Saturday.
Open Sundays 11am - 4pm but this is variable

6) The Curtain Factory Shop
279 HIGH STREET, LINCOLN, LINCOLNSHIRE LN2 1JG
TEL: 01522 522740
Open: 9am - 5pm Monday - Saturday

NORTHWEST ENGLAND AND THE LAKEDISTRICT

The northwest of England may summon up in some minds visions of 'satanic mills' but it is also home to some of Britain's most spectacular scenery. The eastern border of this area is formed by the Pennine hills whilst the western boundary encompasses some of the finest sandy beaches. Finally the northern segment of this area, the Lake District, has been celebrated down the ages by artists and poets, many of whom, like Wordsworth, drew inspiration for their works from the supreme beauty of Cumbria's lakes and fells. Cheek by jowl with all this scenic beauty are the industrial towns of northern Cheshire and Lancashire which means that factory shopping bargains are also never very far away – if you know where to look.

TOUR 1
Ellesmere Port, Chester, Flint and Mostyn

This tour begins at **The Boat Museum,** Ellesmere Port which occupies the historic docks at the junction of the Manchester Ship Canal and Shropshire Union Canal which, at one time, was one of the most important points for the transference of goods from canal to sea-going vessels. There are many floating vessels at the museum from small craft to a 300-ton coaster a lot of which visitors can go aboard to explore. There are also several interesting exhibitions relating to canal and local life and the industrial history of the area

From here it is a very short journey indeed to an outstanding factory shopping complex off junction 10 of the M53 just outside Ellesmere Port. The **Cheshire Oaks** comprises 59 outlets, all selling brand name merchandise at discounted prices. Labels include Paul Costelloe, Timberland, Nike, Liz Claiborne, Levi's, Scotch House, Jeffrey Rogers, Fred Perry, Benetton, Kurt Geiger, Equator luggage, John Partridge countrywear, Edinburgh Crystal, J B Armstrong, Sears womenswear (Richards, Wallis, Warehouse) trading as Collective, Principles/Burton, Tie Rack, Viyella, Fruit of the Loom, Catamini childrenswear, Eminence lingerie, Acced womens and menswear (a French manufacturer), Dim hosiery and lingerie (including Elbeo, Pretty Polly, Playtex, Cacherel), Suits You menswear, James Barry, Sapphire Books, the British Shoe Corporation trading as Famous Footwear, Remington, Lee Cooper, Russell Athletic, Dorothy Perkins, Woods of Windsor, Mexx, Bed & Bath, Daks Simpson, Jaeger, Elegance, The Suit Company, Villeroy & Boch, Suits You, Ravel, Tog 24, Jumpers, Pilot, Toyworld, Helly Hansen, Next to Nothing, Papertree, Joe Bloggs, Jane Shilton and JoKids. There is a children's play area, a Garfunkels restaurant, a McDonalds, and free car parking.

From Cheshire Oaks its a short hop up the M53 to **Chester** itself which, with its combination of old timber-framed buildings, Roman and medieval remains, is one of Britains most appealing cities. You can spend days exploring Chester – with a cathedral, zoo, several museums and a wealth of ancient buildings the visitor here is spoilt for choice. If nothing else, you must visit the Rows, the 13th century covered galleries in Watergate, Eastgate and Bridge St. The Rows are unique to this town which, during the Roman occupation of Britain, was one of their most important strategic bases and headquarters of a legion.

From there carry on to 44 Lower Bridge St where **Something Different,** a permanent discount outlet, is located. Here you can buy, at favourable prices, upmarket ladies clothes, with a lot of day wear from the top end of the high street – names such as Alexon, Louis Feraud, Liberty and Jaeger, amongst others. There is a special events room, a hire section for ballgowns and cocktail dresses. Casual wear is also available with some sports wear including ski clothing. There are no annual sales but there is a special couture designer rail. The shop also runs charity shows at hotels. They also sell a new range of clothes called Saraha.

From Chester a very scenic drive up the A548 coast road overlooking the Dee estuary will bring you to **Flint Castle,** a late 13th century fortification begun by Edward Ist. Its great tower, separated by a moat, is of particular note as it was one of the last circular keeps to be constructed, and part of the walls of the inner bailey and corner towers also remain.

A further 6 miles north west on this road will bring you to Llanerch-y-Mor from where there is a superb view across the sands of the Dee estuary to the Wirral in the east. This is also the home of **Abakhan Fabrics** who are as well known for the emphasis they put on value for money as they are for the huge variety of fabrics, needlecrafts, haberdashery, gifts and knitting yarns that they have gathered from all around the world. The large mill shop complex in Clwyd has baskets of remnant fabrics, wools, yarns and unrivalled selections of fabrics sold by the metre from evening wear, bridal wear and crepe de Chine to curtaining, nets and velvets. Here in this historic building, there are more than ten tonnes of remnant fabrics and 10,000 rolls, all at mill shop prices. Abakhan is able to offer such bargains through bulk buying, or selling clearance lines, job lots and seconds. There is a coffee shop and free parking also at this outlet.

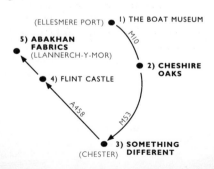

FACTFILE

1) The Boat Museum
SOUTH PIER RD, ELLESMERE PORT, CHESHIRE.
TEL: 0151 355 5017
Open: daily April-October, 10am - 5pm, November-March 11am - 4pm (closed Thursdays and Fridays and 25th & 26th December).
Admission: £4.70 (children £3 OAPs & students £3.60, family ticket £14.50)

2) Cheshire Oaks Designer Outlet Village
KINSEY ROAD, ELLESMERE PORT, SOUTH WIRRAL, CHESHIRE L65 9JJ
TEL: 0151 356 7932.
Open: 10am - 6pm Monday- Saturday, Thursday and Friday 10am - 8pm, 11am - 5pm Sunday and Bank Holidays.

3) Something Different
44 LOWER BRIDGE ST, CHESTER. CH1 1RS
TEL: (01244) 317484.
Open: 9.30 am - 5pm Monday - Saturday

4) Flint Castle
FLINT, CLWYD.
TEL: 01352 733078
Open: At all times. Admission: Free

5) Abakhan Fabrics
COAST RD, MOSTYN, CLWYD. CH8 9DX
TEL: 01745 560312.
Open: 9am - 5.15pm seven days a week, until 8pm on Thursday. The gift, craft and special offer shop is open 9am - 4.30pm on Sunday. The rolls and remnant shop is open Sunday 10.30am - 4.30pm. The coffee shop is open 9am - 5pm

TOUR 2
Colne, Burnley, Samlesbury, Blackpool and Fleetwood

Our tour starts 3 miles east of Colne at **Wycoller Country Park** in the Pennine moorland country of the Brontes. Here there are ancient pack-horse and clapper bridges, 17th century cottages and the ruins of Wycoller Hall which was the model for Ferndean Manor in Charlotte Bronte's 'Jane Eyre'.

Having sampled the sombre moorland that so fired the imagination of this remarkable literary family, a return to Colne and the **Boundary Mill Stores** will stimulate your more mundane appetites. For here is one of the largest clearance stores in Britain, which covers more than 60,000 square feet. As well as a department selling household textiles at discount prices, some of the top end of the high street designer labels are on sale here for both women and men. The women's and men's departments are very extensive - not to mention impressive - and cover the whole range from casual to evening wear, with reductions of between 30% and 50%. There is also a large shoe and a jeans department, a lingerie and nightwear department. Four times a year, there are special sales at which prices are discounted still further. Most of the stock is perfect clearance and ends of lines with the occasional marked seconds. Boundary Mill Stores recently opened its new home furnishings, glass, china and giftware departments adjacent to the original mill, offering quality branded goods at discounted prices. There is free parking, a coffee shop and a restaurant.

From Boundary Mill a quick hop along the M65 will bring you to the **Liberty Mill Shop** at Widow Hill Rd, Burnley. Here you will find Liberty's famous range of exclusive, printed fabrics including the classic Liberty printed cotton Tana Lawn and Varuna wool remnants, as well as ready-to-sew garments, shawls, silk scarves, shirts, ties, gifts and furnishing fabrics. The occasional warehouse sale also features furniture, bedlinen and furnishing fabrics.

From here return to the M65 and head west towards Blackburn and junction 6 where you should exit via the ring road and A677 for Preston. **Samlesbury Hall,** our next stop, is about midway between Blackburn and Preston. The previous house on this site was destroyed by the Scots after Bannockburn and the present marvellously photogenic black and white timbered manor house dates mainly from the

15th and 16th centuries. The surrounding grounds are extensive and at the house there are often sales of antiques and craft items. There are tea rooms and goods on sale to visitors.

From Samlesbury a rather longer drive of around 25 miles via the M6 (northbound) and M55 will take you to Blackpool where at Clifton Rd Retail Park you will find the **K Shoes factory shop.** Clarks International operate a chain of factory shops nationally which specialise in selling discontinued lines and slight sub-standards for children, women and men from Clarks, K Shoes and other famous brands. These shops trade under the name of Crockers, K Shoes Factory shop or Clarks Factory Shop and while not all are physically attached to a shoe factory, these shops are treated as factory shops by the company. Customers can expect to find an extensive range of quality shoes, sandals, walking boots, slippers, trainers, handbags, accessories and gifts, while their major outlets also offer luggage, sports clothing, sports equipment and outdoor clothing. Brands stocked include Clarks, K Shoes, Springer, CICA, Hi-Tec, Puma, Mercury, Dr Martens, Nike, LA Gear, Fila, Mizuno, Slazenger, Weider, Samsonite, Delsey, Antler and Carlton, although not all are sold in every outlet. Discounts are on average 30% off the normal high street price for perfect stock.

Blackpool, of course, has well-documented attractions but there's still plenty of shopping to do if you just carry on a little further north along the A584 coast road to Fleetwood. Here, at Anchorage Rd, is the **Freeport Shopping Village** which contains up to 40 shops, a marina, a US-style diner, and lots of activities for the family. Shops include: 424 Superstore (club football gear), Farah menswear, Tom Sayers menswear, Double Two shirts, Lee jeans, Tick Tock childrenswear, Hallmark cards, Toy World, Sports Unlimited, Honey fashions, Regatta (outdoor clothing), Jane Shilton, Shoe Sellers, Warners lingerie, Ponden Mill (home furnishings), Edinburgh Crystal, Equator luggage, Churchill China, Dorothy Perkins, Next to Nothing, Remington electrical products, Rawhide store leather accessories, London Leathers Direct, The Suit Company, Etcetera reject shop, Royal Stafford and Edinburgh Crystal.

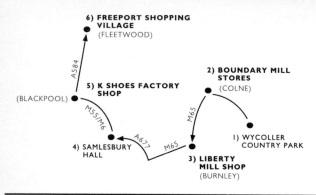

FACTFILE

1) Wycoller Country Park
WYCOLLER, LANCASHIRE
TEL: 01282 863627
Open: Daily all year. Admission: Free

2) Boundary Mill Stores
BURNLEY RD, COLNE, LANCASHIRE. BB8 8LS
TEL: 01282 865229
Open: 10am - 6pm Monday - Friday, 10am - 5pm Saturday and Bank
Holidays, 11am - 5pm Sunday

3) Liberty Mill Shop
LIBERTY DISTRIBUTION CENTRE, WIDOW HILL ROAD, BURNLEY,
LANCASHIRE. BB10 2TJ
TEL: 01282 424600
Open: 10am - 4pm Monday - Friday, 9.30am - 1pm Saturday

4) Samlesbury Hall
PRESTON NEW RD, SAMLESBURY, PRESTON LANCASHIRE PR5 0UP
TEL: (01254) 812010 & 812229
Open: All year Tuesday -Sunday, 11am - 4.30pm closed during
Christmas period
Admission: £2.50 (children 4-16 £1)

5) K Shoes Factory Shop

UNIT 3, CLIFTON ROAD RETAIL PARK, BLACKPOOL, LANCASHIRE
FY4 4RA
TEL: (01253) 699380
Open: 9.30 - 7.30 Monday - Friday, Bank Holidays and Saturday;
10am - 4pm Sunday

6) Freeport Shopping & Leisure Village

ANCHORAGE RD, FLEETWOOD, LANCASHIRE FY7 6AE
TEL: (01253) 877377
Open: 9.30am - 5.30 pm seven days a week.

TOUR 3
Lancaster, Hornby, Cowan Bridge and Kendal

This tour begins in Lancaster where there has been a settlement since
Roman times. Today there are still many fine buildings in the town.
Lancaster Castle on the Castle Hill is still in use today as a courthouse
and prison but it is open to guided tours where it is possible to see the
splendid Shire Hall with its magnificent collection of heraldic shields
portraying the coats of arms of all the sovereigns of England from
Richard the Lionheart onwards. Much of the **Norman Castle** still
remains including the keep built by King John in about 1170. As a
stronghold, the castle with its towers and walls was too much for Robert
The Bruce and his marauding Scottish army when they sacked the town
in 1322 but made no impression on the castle.

Having had your fill of Lancaster's historic past you should conclude
with a visit to the **Standfast Fabric shop** in Caton Rd. This is a genuine
factory shop selling a wide range of well-known designer named fabrics,
which are suitable for all soft furnishings, at discounted prices. Stocks
vary according to factory production and all fabrics are seconds with
prices ranging from £5 to £8 per metre. They always stock plenty of
pieces for cushion covers and patchwork from 15p each to £3 for a small
sackful. Usually they also have some fabrics on special offer, ranging
from £1.50 per metre to £7 a metre. None of the fabric is flame retar-
dant but once treated, it can be used for upholstery. The shop also

stocks dress linen in a wide range of colours at £1.50 a metre.

From Lancaster there is a picturesque drive north east up the Lune valley along the A683. There is a superb view of Hornby Castle from this road which was built by Sir Edward Stanley, an English knight who, in 1513, had fought under the Earl of Surrey in the great victory over the Scots at Flodden Field. As thanks-giving for his safe return from this battle Sir Edward built the octagonal tower of St Margaret's Church in Hornby. Continuing on on the A683 and A65 (northbound) you will pick up signs for Cowan Bridge. Here, at Bridge Mill, you will find **Jumpers,** a factory shop that produces a wide range of sweaters for men and women – all at discount prices.

From here continue on this attractive drive north west on the A65 towards Kendal. As you come into Kendal on the A591 you will pick up signs for **K Village Factory Shopping Centre** which has eight outlets including Crabtree & Evelyn, Denby Pottery, Dartington Crystal, Farah Menswear, Jumpers, The Baggage Factory, The Sports Factory and a giant K Shoes factory shop selling a wide range of labels from Clarks, Jumpers, Farah, Laura Ashley, Delsey, Cica, and Antler. There is also a heritage centre, a 150-seater restaurant, a coffee shop and free parking.

From here it is no distance to **Kendal** the gateway of the great lakes of Cumbria. In the town itself there is much to see amongst which is the museum on Station Rd which deals with the archaeology and natural history of the lakes and has a gallery devoted to Alfred Wainwright the author and great walker of the Lake District who was honorary clerk to the Museum.

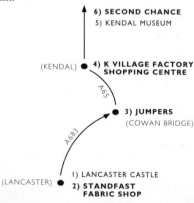

FACTFILE

1) Lancaster Castle
SHIRE HALL, CASTLE PARADE, LANCASTER
TEL: 01524 64998
Open: Easter-October daily 10.30am (first tour) - 4pm (last tour).
Because of Court sessions always telephone to check tour times except
in August.
Admission: £2.50 (children & OAPs £1.75)

2) Standfast Fabric Factory Shop
CATON RD, LANCASTER LA1 3PA
TEL: 01524 64334
Open: 9.30am - 1pm Monday - Friday, 10am - 12.30pm Saturday

3) Jumpers
BRIDGE MILL, COWAN BRIDGE, CARNFORTH, LANCASHIRE.
LA6 2HS
TEL: 01524 272726
Open: 10am - 4pm seven days a week in summer. (Phone to check
opening details).

4) K Village Factory Shopping
NETHERFIELD, KENDAL, CUMBRIA. LA9 7DA
(NR JUNCTION 36 OF M6)
TEL: 01539 721892
Open 9.30am - 6pm Monday - Friday, 9am - 6pm Saturday,
11am - 5pm Bank Holidays and Sundays.

5) Kendal Museum
STATION RD, KENDAL, CUMBRIA LH9 6BT
TEL: 01539 721374
Open: 10.30am - 4pm 17th Feb - 31st March, 10.30am - 5pm1st
April - 31st October, 10.30am - 4pm 1st November - December.
Closed 23rd December for Christmas period.
Admission: £2.50 (children £1, OAPs £1.90)

6) Second Chance
27 ALL HALLOWS LANE, KENDAL, CUMBRIA LA9 4JH.
TEL: 01539 740414.
Open 9am - 5.30pm Monday - Saturday

YORKSHIRE, HUMBERSIDE AND NORTH EAST ENGLAND

Yorkshire, Northumberland and Durham are counties that provide a wide cross-section of scenery from the rolling grainlands of the Wolds, to the limestone crags of the Pennines and the vast sandy beaches of the Northumbrian coast. This is also an area steeped in ecclesiastical, military and industrial history and there are many fascinating remnants of this past intact and preserved for posterity in settings whose beauty is a challenge to the most creative imaginations.

TOUR 1
Harrogate, Fountains Abbey, Lightwater Valley, Newby Hall and Boroughbridge

Our tour starts in the attractive spa town of Harrogate in North Yorkshire that as late as the 1950s was still attracting large numbers of people to take the 'cure' of its sulphur waters. It has handsome streets, gardens and squares and rows of pretty and interesting shops in its commercial centre. Amongst these, at 41 Tower St, is **Waltons Mill Shop** a high street retail outlet which sells international designer fabrics with the emphasis on high class designs with a difference. More unusually, they also stock a vast range of quality trimmings, cords, bullions, tassels, tie-backs, etc. Regular customers really do describe the shop as an Aladdin's cave, with its tapestries, handmade quilts, Egyptian cotton bedding, throws, cushions and traditional household textiles. Those who have tried the famous Knaresborough linen dishcloth vow never to use anything else again. Most of the stock is overmakes, bankrupt merchandise, bought from the US or imported from all over the world. Tucked away, you have to take the A61 Leeds road into Harrogate, and take the first right hand turn after the Prince of Wales roundabout at the longterm car park sign. The shop is 200 yards up on the left hand side.

Another Harrogate discount outlet well worth a visit is **Labels For Less** at 16 Princes St which is the designer and quality fashion clearance outlet for Harrogate's leading fashion store, Hewletts. At Labels for Less, you will find an extensive range of sensational design houses at a fraction of their original price - all year round. Basler, Betty Barclay, Gerry Weber, Bianca, Fink Separa and Ara are just a few of the names on offer. Big savings in fashion, but no reduction in style is the Labels for Less motto where, in addition to regular discounts of up to 50%, there are often also outstanding seasonal offers. All merchandise has previously been sold at full price within the main Hewletts store and comprises mainly end of season lines. All merchandise is new and the majority of items are from the previous year's collections.

Leaving Harrogate via the A61 northbound travel as far as Ripon where you should take the B6265 west for about three miles to **Fountains Abbey** and **Studley Royal.** The ruins of the 12th century **Cistercian Abbey** stand in the lovely valley of the River Skell and, set amongst the landscaped splendour of William Aislabie's gardens, are truly one of the most evocative and atmospheric sights in the whole of the British Isles. There is so much of the original abbey left that the visitor has to engage in very little of the 'piecing together' that is required at other sites and the ruins give a comprehensive insight into life at a medieval monastery. The surrounding gardens include formal water gardens, ornamental temples and follies and are bordered by a large deer park.

From Fountains Abbey a short drive back up to Ripon and four miles north up the A6108 will then bring you to **Lightwater Valley Theme Park and Village.** The theme park offers rides and amusements for all the family but, just as importantly in the context of this book, some of the property has been converted to factory shop retailing. You can visit the shopping village free, without visiting the theme park which makes a charge. There are various factory shops on site selling brand names such as Windsmoor, Planet, James Barry, Tula, Jane Shilton, Edinburgh Crystal, Hornsea Pottery, Accord Bedlinen. The pottery shop has plenty of ceramics and kitchen utensils to choose from, while the crystal shop has glasses, decanters, giftware and bowls. There are two enormous "warehouses" with masses of fashion for women and men, bedlinen, duvets, shoes, perfume, cookware, suitcases and cosmetics. There will eventually be parking for 4,000 cars and 120 coaches, a market square, coffee shops, food shops, a wine bar, covered garden centre, visitors farm and trout pond.

Heading for Newby Hall will take you back to Ripon on the A6108 where a stopover at the ancient and handsome 13th century cathedral will well repay the effort. Heading out of Ripon once again on the B6265 will then bring you shortly to signs for **Newby Hall.** The late 17th century hall posesses a splendid interior that is another of Robert Adam's famous achievements and contains a renowned collection of Italian statues and Gobelin tapestries. The gardens are as beautiful as the house and possess a shop, restaurant, childrens' adventure garden and miniature railway.

Our final stop on this tour takes us just a couple of miles further on on the B6265 to Boroughbridge where the **Boroughbridge Trading Co** is situated at St James Square. Sister company to the Downton Trading Company in Wiltshire (see South West), this shop sells other top-name small company's seconds, overmakes, discounted and discontinued lines. The number of companies changes constantly but there are usually about 40 or 50 selling different goods in the shop at any one time, with a changeover of stock every three months. These include hand-painted porcelain boxes; hand lacquered tablemats, trays and wastepaper baskets; tapestry stools; limited editions, paintings and prints; drawing room china; seconds in high quality photograph frames, clocks, cartoon frames, and greetings cards from Bryn Parry; oleographs; designer fabric nursery bags; and silk ties and braces; as well as candles, leather goods, table lamps and shades, drawing room furniture, plant pot holders, silver for the dining room table, American soft toys, conservatory furniture and accessories, kitchen pottery, leather-bound photograph albums, bulletin boards, christmas decorations (in season), crystal glass and victorian paintings. Everything is colour coded in four categories so you can tell whether you're buying a second, discounted, overmake or a perfect but discontinued line, and prices reflect that.

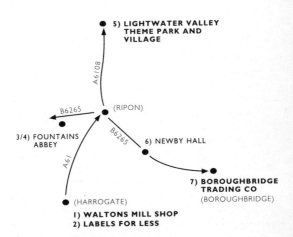

FACTFILE

1) Waltons Mill Shop
41 TOWER STREET, HARROGATE, NORTH YORKSHIRE. HG1 1HS
TEL: 01423 520980
Open 10am - 5pm Monday - Saturday

2) Labels For Less
16 PRINCES STREET, HARROGATE. HG1 1NH
TEL: (01423) 567436
Open: 9.15am - 5.15pm Tuesday - Saturday

3) Fountains Abbey & Studley Royal Water Gardens
RIPON, NR HARROGATE, NORTH YORKSHIRE HG4 3DY
TEL: 01765 608888
Open: all year. Abbey & garden 10am - 5pm January - March,
November and December daily (except 24th and 25th December and
Friday November - January). or dusk if earlier;
10am - 7pm April - September.
Admission: £4 (children £2) family ticket £8

5) Lightwater Valley Theme Park & Village
NORTH STAINLEY, NORTH YORKSHIRE
TEL: 01765 635321 OR 635334
Open: 10am - 5pm seven days a week all year round
Admission: low season 30th March - 27th July, £8.95 (under 1.33
metres in height £6.95, OAPs £6.95, children under 4 years free).
High season £9.95 (under 1.33 metres in height £7.95, OAPs £7.95,
children under 4 years free).
Closes 4pm on 5th and 6th July 1996 for a special event.

6) Newby Hall & Gardens
RIPON, NORTH YORKSHIRE HG4 5AE
TEL: 01423 322583
Open: April - September, Tuesday - Sundays and Bank Holidays;
Gardens 11am - 5.30pm; **House** 12 noon - 5pm. Last admission
5pm (gardens) 4.30pm (house)
Admission: house and gardens £5.40 (children and disabled £3.20,
OAPs £4.50. Gardens £3.80 (children and disabled £2.50, OAPs
£3.30); house and gardens family ticket (2 adults plus 2 children)
£16.20, gardens only family ticket £11.50

7) The Boroughbridge Trading Company
ST JAMES SQ, BOROUGHBRIDGE, NORTH YORKSHIRE.
YO5 9AW
TEL: 01423 324584
Open: 9.30am - 5pm Monday - Saturday

TOUR 2
*Burton Agnes Hall, Nafferton, Gt Driffield,
Skipsea and Hornsea*

Burton Agnes Hall in the village of that name midway between
Bridlington and Driffield on the A166 is our starting point on this tour.
The hall is a striking Tudor house constructed of red brick with a stone
trim and was built in 1598 by Sir Henry Griffith. The house is full of
magnificent china, furniture and paintings collected over the last 400
years and has some especially memorable features particularly the beautiful Long Gallery and oak panelled drawing-room. It has a walled
garden with maze and woodland garden walks as well as a scented
garden for the blind and the old hall (which the Tudor hall replaced) is
still very much in evidence.

If we travel west from here on the A166 we come to the village of
Nafferton. Here, of particular interest to those with children, is situated
at Rectory Farm, Middle St an outlet of the **Nippers** franchise. Nippers,
the nursery equipment and toy specialists, started with a very clever and
simple idea and have now created an award-winning chain of franchises.
The company operates from converted barns on farms around the

country, offering easy parking, no queues, and personal service. This is on top of competitive prices on prams, cots, pushchairs, car seats, outdoor play equipment and toys. Prices are low partly because they operate from farms, with none of the overheads of traditional retail outlets, and partly because the successful growth of a number of branches means it can now buy in bulk and negotiate good deals. Customers can try out the merchandise and the children can see the animals, mostly sheep, chickens and pigs. Familiar brand names are on sale at all the branches, including Britax, Maclaren and Bebe Confort, Fisher-Price and Little Tikes. You can try out the car seats in your car and there is usually a pram/pushchair repair service on site.

From here it is a couple of miles into Driffield where there is an **I J Dewhirst factory shop** at 42 Middle Street North. Dewhirst's sell a wide range of men's, women's and children's clothing including men's suits, jackets, shirts and trousers, and jackets, blouses, skirts and trousers for women and girls.

Taking the B1249 will take you on a winding but attractive route to Skipsea. Here you can stop and peruse the remaining earthworks of the 11th century **Norman motte and bailey castle.** Once the base of Drogo de Brevere, a Flemish adventurer who had married a relative of William The Conqueror, it was seized by the Crown after he had killed his wife and fled to the continent. The castle was eventually demolished by Henry III after it had become a centre of rebellion. around 1220.

Carrying on south about another 6 miles on the B1242 will then take you to Hornsea where the **Freeport Village** was one of the very first factory shopping villages in the UK. At Hornsea Freeport there are leisure attractions such as Birds of Prey, The Yorkshire Car Collection, the Model Village and an outdoor adventure playground There is also about two dozen shops where you can buy brand name discounted goods. Labels include Daks Simpson, Edinburgh Crystal, Laura Ashley, Wrangler, Windsmoor, Planet, Genesis, Berkertex, Aquascutum, Jersey Pearl, Tom Sayers menswear, Tog 24, Sports Unlimited, Churchill China and Warners.

FACTFILE

1) Burton Agnes Hall
BURTON AGNES, HUMBERSIDE YO25 0ND
TEL: 01262 490324
Open: 11am - 5pm daily April-October
Admission: hall & grounds: £3.50 (children £2, OAPs £3).
Grounds Only: £1.80 (children 80p, OAPs £1.50)

2) Nippers
RECTORY FARM, MIDDLE STREET, NAFFERTON, DRIFFIELD,
EAST YORKSHIRE YO25 0JS
TEL: 01377 240689. FAX 01377 240687
Open: Tuesday - Friday 10am - 4pm, Saturday 10am - 5pm, Sunday
12 noon - 4pm closed Monday

3) I J Dewhirst
42 MIDDLE STREET NORTH, DRIFFIELD, NORTH HUMBERSIDE
YO25 7SS
TEL: 01377 256209.
Open: 9am - 5.30pm Monday - Friday, 9am - 5pm Saturday

4) Skipsea Castle
SKIPSEA, NORTH HUMBERSIDE
Maintained by English Heritage, Open any reasonable time,
Admission: Free

5) Hornsea Freeport
HORNSEA, NORTH HUMBERSIDE. HU18 1UT
TEL: **01964 534211**
Open: 10am - 5pm seven days a week including Bank Holidays

TOUR 3
Spennymoor, Darlington, Middlesbrough and Hartlepool

This tour covers an essentially industrial part of the North east but there
is plenty to see of cultural and historical interest in a part of England
that was one of the cradles of the Industrial Revolution – an important,
coal, iron and steel producing centre as well as the area that witnessed
the birth of the railway.

The tour starts at the **Black & Decker** service centre at Spennymoor.
Here you can obtain reconditioned tools and acccessories from the
famous Black & Decker range, all with full B&D warranty. This is
essentially an after-sales service with a retail outlet. All the reconditioned
tools come under the Gold Seal label. Often, stock consists of goods
returned from the shops because of damaged packaging or are part of a
line which is being discontinued. There are usually lots of seasonal
special offers. Reconditioned lawnmowers from £27-£150; drills, £37;
jigsaws, £22.99.

From Spennymoor motor south on the A167 to Darlington where at
North Rd Station the **Darlington Railway Centre & Museum** is
based. In September 1825 the world's first railway opened between
Stockton and Darlington and the most famous exhibit at the museum
is "Locomotion" which pulled the first passenger train and was built by
Robert Stephenson. There are several other early locomotives along with
an early 19th century carriage and coal wagon.

Also in Darlington at 1 East Row is **Seymour's Warehouse.**
Seymour's is Darlington's longest-established household linen store,

attracting customers from all the surrounding areas and further afield. They stock an amazing selection of household linens including ranges by Dorma, Christy, Hamilton McBride, Nimbus, Rectella, Sheridan, Snuggledown, Broomhill, all perfect and at extremely competitive prices. Established over 35 years, this is a family owned and run business offering personal service, special clearance lines, ready-made curtains and a curtain ordering service. Linens stocked include shower curtains, bath sets, cushions, pillows, duvet covers, flannelette sheets, bedspreads, travel rugs, a wide selection of duvets, blankets, children's quilt covers, towelling robes and much more. The stock changes constantly with daily deliveries. Efforts will always be made to acquire an item which is not in stock. The shop also stocks chainstore seconds and factory mill seconds from firms such as Early's of Witney.

A short journey east along the A66 will then take you to Middlesbrough where at Stewart Park, Marton, just off the A172, is the **Captain Cook Birthplace Museum.** Captain Cook was born in Marton in 1728 and the Museum has exhibits illustrating his early life and also his famous voyages of discovery in the Pacific Ocean. There is a conservatory of tropical plants, a spacious park and some animal and wildfowl attractions.

The final visit on this tour combines some fascinating sightseeing with a wonderful shopping opportunity as you travel north from Middlesbrough along the A172 and A178 to Hartlepool via the golden sands of Seaton Carew which is passed on the way.

At Hartlepool you should head for the Marina and **Jacksons Landing.** There you will find an indoor factory shopping centre with twenty-four outlets selling brand name items from companies such as Edinburgh Crystal, Royal Brierley, Wrangler and Equator Luggage. Shops such as Clinkards sell Bally, Clark's and Kickers Footwear; there is also Jane Shilton handbags; Jokids sells childrenswear; Toy World features many of the leading brand names such as Tomy, Fisher-Price and Lego; James Barry has a selection of men's suits, shirts, and jackets; Bookscene sells jigsaws, stationery, posters; Tog 24 sells leisurewear; Honey offers a range of affordable knitwear, T-shirts and leggings, including Honey Plus for sizes 18-24; Chas N Whillans, Scottish branded wool specialist, sells famous branded quality lambswool and cashmere including Lyle & Scott and Pringle; Hallmark sells half-price celebration and Christmas cards, wrapping paper, and stuffed toys; and Tom Sayers sells a range of menswear; while Treasure Island sells specialised gifts from Hartlepool. Recent new openings include Benetton,

Joe Bloggs and Fruit Of The Loom T-shirts and sweatshirts for all the family. Hartlepool Marina hosts a recreated historic quay and harbours HMS Trincomalee, the oldest British warship still afloat, and is also the site of the new Hartlepool Museum with its interactive fighting ships section and a replica seventeenth century children's play area. There is free parking adjacent to the centre, a coffee shop, restaurant overlooking the marina, and baby changing and disabled facilities.

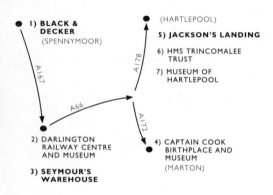

FACTFILE

1) Black & Decker Service Centre
GREEN LANE, SPENNYMOOR, CO DURHAM. DL16 6JG
TEL: 01388 422429
Open: 8.30am - 5pm Monday, Tuesday, Thursday, Friday, 9.30am - 5 pm Wednesday, 8.30am - 12.30pm Saturday.

2) Darlington Railway Centre & Museum
NORTH ROAD STATION, DARLINGTON, CO DURHAM DL3 6ST
TEL: 01325 460532
Open: daily 10am - 5pm (closed Christmas and New Year);
Admission: £1.90 (children 95p, OAPs £1.40)

3) Seymour's Warehouse
1 EAST ROW, DARLINGTON, CO DURHAM. DL1 5PZ
TEL: 01325 355272
Open 9am - 5pm Monday - Saturday

4) Captain Cook Birthplace Museum
STEWART PARK, MARTON, MIDDLESBROUGH, CLEVELAND TS7 6AS
TEL: 01642 311211
Open: all year, summer: Tuesday - Sunday, 10am - 5.30pm;
winter, 9am - 4pm. Last ticket 30 mins before closing
(closed 25th, 26th Dec & and January 1st)
Admission: £1.30 (children & OAPs 65p)

5) Jacksons Landing Hartlepool Factory Outlet
HARTLEPOOL MARINA, HARTLEPOOL, CLEVELAND. TS24 OXN
TEL: 01429 866989 INFORMATION LINE.
Open: 10am - 6pm Monday - Saturday, 11am - 5pm Sunday and
Bank Holidays, closed 25th, 26th December and 1st January.

6) HMS Trincomalee Trust
JACKSON'S DOCK, HARTLEPOOL, CLEVELAND TS24 0SQ
TEL: 01429 223193
Open: all year, Monday - Friday 1.30pm - 4.30pm, Saturday, Sunday
and Bank Holidays 10am - 5pm
(closed Christmas & New Year)
Admission: £2.50 (children and OAPs £1.50)

7) Museum of Hartlepool
JACKSON DOCK, HARTLEPOOL, CLEVELAND TS24 0XF
TEL: 01429 266522
Open: all year, 10am - 6pm seven days a week (closed 25th, 26th
December and 1st January)
Admission: free

TOUR 4
Jarrow, Blyth, Ashington and Alnwick

This tour starts in an area that is now part of a great industrial port and conurbation but is also the site of one of the great centres of English ecclesiastical history. **St Paul's Church** at Church Bank, Jarrow is now all that remains of the monastery where the Venerable Bede worked and worshipped until his death in 735. This site is considered to be 'the cradle of English learning' for it was here that Bede wrote the 'Ecclesiastical History of the English People' and many other books that represented the collected learning of his time. The church now incorporates 'Bede's World' where the story of the monastery is told and a museum.

Also in Jarrow, on the Bede Industrial Estate, is the factory shop of one of the country's most famous clothing manufacturer's, **Barbour.** Here you can buy their famous waterproof waxed jackets and outdoor wear, all of which are seconds or discontinued lines, at discounts of 10%-25%. Jackets comes in fifteen different styles from short to full-length and in various colours, but you may not find the style, colour and size you want as quantities vary. There are also shooting jackets, tweed hats and caps, linings for coats, bags, waxed trousers, waders and some children's waxed jackets.

From Jarrow then take the A19 and A189 north to Blyth. here, at the Kitty Brewster Industrial Estate, is situated another leading brands factory shop – **Burberry.** Here there are seconds and overmakes of the famous name raincoats and duffle coats as well as accessories such as the distinctive umbrellas, scarves and handbags. It also sells children's duffle coats, knitwear and shirts, as well as some of the Burberry range of food: jams, biscuits, tea, coffee and chocolate. All carry the Burberry label and are about one third off the normal retail price.

If you need some fresh air and exercise, **Blyth's** three-mile stretch of sands provides an excellent opportunity, otherwise you can press on north up the A189 to Ashington where the **Dewhirst factory shop** is located at the North Seaton Industrial Estate. The shop offers a wide range of men's, women's and children's clothes including men's suits, jackets, shirts, trousers; women's jackets, blouses, skirts and trousers; girl's dresses, blouses, trousers, skirts and jackets and boy's shirts, trousers, jackets and much much more.

From here you can finally break out of industrial Northumberland by taking the A189 and A1068 25 miles through country villages to the charming market town of **Alnwick.** The cobblestones, narrow streets and passageways are reminiscent of a bygone age and the castle, home of the Dukes of Northumberland for seven centuries, is so grand as to have been known in Victorian times as the 'Windsor of the North'. Within, it is a treasure house of fine furniture and paintings containing works by Titian, Van Dyke and Canaletto and there are some fascinating exhibitions of British and Roman relics along with the Northumberland Fusiliers Regimental Museum.

Walking around Alnwick is a pleasure and while there, if you are an outdoor type, you should drop in at the **House of Hardy factory shop** in Willowburn. House of Hardy products go to all the best department stores in London at a price that befits their quality and reputation. Here, you can obtain ends of lines of many of these including waxed jackets, jumpers, fly vests, tops and trousers, countrywear bags, fishing rods, reels, and lines. There is also a bargain basement with own brand items on sale at discounts of about 50%.

5) ALNWICK CASTLE

6) HOUSE OF HARDY FACTORY SHOP

A1068

(ASHINGTON) 4) DEWHIRST FACTORY SHOP

A189

(BLYTH) 3) BURBERRY

A19/A189

(JARROW) 1) BEDE'S WORLD

2) BARBOUR

FACTFILE

1) Bede's World

CHURCH BANK, JARROW, TYNE & WEAR NE32 3DY
TEL: 0191 489 2106
Open: all year, 10am - 5.30pm Tuesday - Saturday and Bank Holiday
Mondays, Sunday 2.30pm - 5.30pm April - October; 11am - 4.30pm
Tuesday - Saturday, 2.30pm - 5.30pm Sunday November - March.
(closed 25th December to 1st January).
Church open 10am - 4.30pm April-October; 11am - 4.30pm Monday
- Saturday and 2.30pm - 4.30pm Sunday November - March
Admission: Church: free.
Admission to Bede's World: £2.50 (children, OAPs, UB40 and
disabled £1.25), family ticket 2 adults and 2 children £6,
unemployed £4.

2) J. Barbour & Sons Ltd

CUSTOMER SERVICE BUILDING, BEDE INDUSTRIAL ESTATE,
SIMONSIDE, JARROW, TYNE & WEAR. NE34 9PG
TEL: 0191 455 4444
Open: 10am - 5pm, Monday - Friday, 9am - 12 noon Saturday

3) Burberry Factory Shop

KITTY BREWSTER INDUSTRIAL ESTATE, BLYTH, NORTHUMBERLAND.
NE24 4RG
TEL: 01670 352524
Open: 10am - 3.30pm Monday - Thursday, 10am - 3pm Friday,
9.30am - 12.30pm Saturday

4) Dewhirst Ltd Factory Shop

NEWBIGGIN RD, NORTH SEATON INDUSTRIAL ESTATE,
ASHINGTON, NORTHUMBERLAND NE63 0YB
TEL: 01670 813493
Open: 9am - 5.30pm Monday - Friday, 9am - 5pm Saturday,
10.30am - 4.30pm Sunday

5) Alnwick Castle
ALNWICK, NORTHUMBERLAND NE66 1NQ
TEL: 01665 510777 & (WEEKENDS) 603942
Open: Easter-mid-October, daily 11am - 5pm, closed Fridays last
admission 4.30pm
Admission: £4.70 (children £2.50, OAPs & students £4.20). Grounds
only: £2.50

6) House of Hardy Factory Shop Museum and Country Store
WILLOW BURN, ALNWICK, NORTHUMBERLAND. NE66 2PF
TEL: 01665 602771
Open: 9am - 5pm Monday - Friday, 10am - 5pm Saturday, 1.30pm -
5pm Sunday from April - October.

SCOTLAND

Although the Scots have been traditionally divided into Highland and Lowland Scots there is, in truth, very little 'lowland' in the whole country. There is virtually nowhere in Scotland where you are not at least in the shadow of hills or mountains. The hills in the southern part of Scotland below the line adjoining Glasgow and Edinburgh are, it is true, on the whole lower and less dramatic than those north of this line but there is still plenty of grandeur about the scenery in the Southern Uplands where rushing streams at the head of dramatic, glaciated 'U-shaped' valleys eventually transform themselves into powerful and imposing rivers such as the Tweed and the Nith. Further north, in the Highlands, some of the most dramatic scenery imaginable is formed by the dramatic confluence of mountains, sea and sky much of which can be enjoyed from roads mercifully free from traffic and congestion. And amidst all this, if you know where to go, you can find some of the best of Scottish manufacture at the keenest of prices.

TOUR 1
Jedburgh, Hawick, Selkirk, Traquair House

We start our tour in Jedburgh, a historic town not ten miles from the border with England and, as such, the scene of much bloody strife over the centuries. **Jedburgh Abbey,** founded as an Augustinian Priory in 1118, has borne witness to much of this and indeed has been sacked and rebuilt many times. Surprisingly, it now stands as the most complete of the border monasteries and a fine example of Saxon and early Gothic architecture.

From Jedburgh the B6358 and A698 provide an inspiring drive down Teviotdale to Hawick where, in an area renowned for its wool production, there are two splendid shopping opportunities. The first visit is to **Short & Robertson's Cashmere Factory Shop** at Unit 17, the Laidlaw Centre where you can obtain designer and classic knitwear in 100% cashmere for women and men, as made for leading stores and couture houses worldwide. Belinda Robertson has an international reputation for designing classics with a twist, and in January 1993, won the NatWest 1992 Export Award. She has a showroom in Edinburgh as well as the factory shop in Hawick which offer ends of ranges, samples and over-runs all sold at discount prices, usually between 25-50% off retail prices. All garments are designed and manufactured in Scotland. Accessories include capes, scarves and gloves.

Your other stop should be at the **Hawick Cashmere Company Factory Shop** at Trinity Mills, Duke St. Here they manufacture cashmere knitwear for top department stores and sell seconds and ends of lines at below retail prices. You will find cashmere and silk, lambswool sweaters, scarves, capes, cardigans, dresses, skirts and gloves. Also there are bargain baskets of cardigans and sweaters from £15

From Hawick, around a 12 mile drive along the A7 as it twists its way northwards through the Southern Uplands will bring you to Selkirk. At Halliwells Close, Market Place (just off the A7) is **Halliwell's House Museum,** Selkirk's oldest surviving dwelling. This has been restored as a period home and ironmonger's shop and contains an exhibition illustrating the town's development.

There is a shopping stop at Selkirk too at **Gardiner of Selkirk's factory shop** at The Tweedmills. Here the factory shop sells textiles: mixed tweeds at £8 a yard, Shetland wool at 35p an ounce, men's pyjamas, socks, shirts (£9.95-£10.95), wool jumpers £20-£25, skirts,

£29.95, jackets, £75, scarves, £2.95 and £3.95, tartan rugs at £19.50, woollen rugs, £8.95-£14.95. Best buys are the tweeds and rugs.

Also on the outskirts of Selkirk near the Riverside Industrial Estate is the **Claridge Mills factory shop** which manufactures fashion fabric for some of the top international designers including Ralph Lauren, Donna Karan, Gucci, Valentino, Chanel, Dior, Perry Ellis, Armani and Worth. The tiny mill shop stocks not only the fabric but also overmakes of some of the items made from the material at factory prices. These include capes, blanket jackets, waistcoats, rugs and carpets in luxury silks and cashmere.

From here it is only a few miles west up the A72 to **Traquair House** which is one mile south of Innerleithen on the B709. This house dates from the 10th century and claims to be the oldest inhabited house in Scotland. Twenty seven Scottish and English Kings have stayed here and it is strongly associated with both Mary Queen of Scots and the 18th century Jacobite rebellions. The Bear gates were closed in 1745 not to be re-opened it is said until a Stuart is monarch once again. The house contains a marvellous collection of historical artefacts and you can purchase its own Traquair ale brewed in its 18th century brewhouse.

FACTFILE

1) Jedburgh Abbey
4-5 ABBEY BRIDGEND, JEDBURGH, ROXBURGHSHIRE
TEL: 0131 668 8800
Open: all year 9.30am - 6.30pm Monday - Saturday, 2pm - 6.30pm
Sunday, April - September; 9.30am - 4.30pm Monday - Saturday,
2pm - 4.30pm Sunday, October - March (closed 25th, 26th
December and 1st, 2nd January)
Admission: £2.50 (children £1, OAPs £1.50)

2) Short & Robertson's Cashmere Factory Shop
UNIT 17, LAIDLAW CENTRE, HAWICK TD9 7DS
TEL: 01450 377648
Open: 9am - 4.30pm Monday - Friday.
Open Saturday by appointment

3) Hawick Cashmere Co Ltd
TRINITY MILLS, DUKE STREET, HAWICK. TD9 9QA
TEL: 01450 372510
Open: 10am - 5pm Monday - Friday

4) Halliwells House Museum
MARKET PLACE, SELKIRK TD7
TEL: 01750 720096
Open: 10am - 5pm Monday - Saturday, April-October,
(July and August until 6pm); 2pm - 4pm Sunday.
Admission: free

5) Gardiner of Selkirk Factory Shop
TWEED MILLS, SELKIRK.TD7 5DZ
TEL:01750 20283
Open: 9am - 5pm Monday - Saturday in summer,
10am - 4pm in winter.

6) Claridge Mills Ltd Shop
RIVERSIDE, NR RIVERSIDE INDUSTRIAL ESTATE (OFF A72 BETWEEN
GALASHIELS AND PEEBLES). SELKIRK TD7 5DU
TEL: 01750 20300
Open: 9am - 4.45pm Monday - Friday

7) Traquair House

TRAQUAIR, NR INNERLEITHEN, PEEBLESHIRE
TEL: 01896 830323 & 830785
Open: 6 April- 30th September daily, 12.30pm - 5.30
(ex July & August 10.30am - 5.30pm). Last admission 5pm.
October Friday - Sunday 2pm - 5pm.
Grounds open April - September 10.30am - 5.30pm.
Admission: £3.80 (children £1.80 OAPs £3.30 Family ticket £10.00)

TOUR 2
Penicuik, Roslin Chapel, East Kilbride,
Giffnock, Alexandria and Loch Lomond

This tour starts at the **Edinburgh Crystal Visitors centre** at the Eastfield Industrial Estate off the A701 on the outskirts of Penicuik. Here you can take tours of the factory where the famous crystal is made and witness the various stages in the glassmaking process. You can also, of course, visit the factory shop where a wide range of crystalware from wine glasses and vases to tumblers and decanters are purchasable. The shop sells firsts and seconds of crystal from one third off the normal price. There are also special promotional lines at discount prices up to 70% off seconds.

Carrying on on the A701/703 in the direction of Edinburgh for about a mile and you will pick up signs for Roslin and Bonnyrigg on the A6094. At Roslin is the famous **Rosslyn Chapel** founded in 1446 and one of Scotland's most precious architectural inheritances. At the behest of its founder, Sir William Sinclair, the chapel was worked on by craftsmen from all over Europe and is full of the most intricate and detailed stone carving, the 'Apprentice Pillar' perhaps being the finest example of this. The chapel is virtually unique in the country, having no other real architectural counterpart and it is fortunate that it has been so well preserved over the generations.

From Roslin go back to the A701 and head north for Edinburgh and then west via the A720, M8, A8 and A725 for East Kilbride just south of Glasgow. Here, at the Kingsgate Retail Park, is the **Big L factory outlet.** This outlet is devoted to selling seconds and ends of lines of Levi's merchandise, and is well worth a visit. All the clothes, which includes the full range of shirts, sweatshirts, jackets, jeans, and cords, are top quality although there may be slight flaws, but please note that all the tabs are cut off every item before it gets to the shop. There is a Fruit of the Loom factory shop next door, making double the reason for a visit.

Carrying on west up the A726 will bring you to Giffnock where you may want to pay a visit to **Q Mark** on Braidholm Rd which is Scotland's biggest discount clothing warehouse for women, men and children and offers top quality fashions at up to 50% off normal high street prices. All garments are good quality seconds, overmakes or cancelled contracts but with their labels cut out. Regular stock deliveries ensure a constant selection of new styles - often recognised in famous chain stores, but always at ridiculously low prices. Q Mark operate a once-a-year membership fee of £5. All prices are subject to VAT and charged at point of sale.

From Giffnock it is only about a mile to **Pollok Country Park** where the famous Burrell Collection is housed. The collection contains ancient Egyptian alabaster, Chinese ceramics and jade, stained glass, tapestries, silver, needlework, and paintings and sculptures by such greats as Bellini, Rembrandt, Manet, Degas and Cezanne. The specially designed gallery is situated in a 360 acre park which contains waterside and woodland trails and also Pollok House which was left to the city along with a remarkable collection of Spanish paintings by artists such as Goya and El Greco.

From here head north into Glasgow where you will soon pick up signs for the A82 and Dumbarton. Head north west along the A82 through Dumbarton and through Alexandria where you will eventually pick up signs for the Lomond Industrial Estate. The **Antartex village visitor centre** is situated here and there is a sheepskin factory and craft workshops where you can watch sheepskin jackets being made, pottery and jewellery and glass engraving taking place. The factory shop sells sheepskin and leather jackets, slippers, gloves and woollens at very good prices and there is often a sale in the shop with plenty of real bargains.

Here, of course, you are very near to the fabled beauty of **Loch Lomond** which you reach by continuing north up the A82 for about two miles. The largest of the Scottish lochs, it is considered by many to be the most beautiful and the journey up the A82 as it twists and turns along its eastern shore is a very rewarding experience.

FACTFILE

1) Edinburgh Crystal Visitor Centre
EASTFIELD INDUSTRIAL ESTATE, PENICUIK, MIDLOTHIAN
EH26 8HB
TEL: 01968 675128
Open: 9am - 5pm Monday - Saturday, 11am - 5pm Sunday
Factory Tours: 9am - 3.30pm Monday - Friday (closed 25th, 26th, 27th December and 1st , 2nd January) April - September factory topurs between 11am - 2.30pm Saturday and Sunday.
Admission: (for factory tours £2, OAPs £1) NB No children under 8 years old allowed on factory tours.

2) Rosslyn Chapel
ROSLIN, MIDLOTHIAN
TEL: 0131 440 2159
Open: 10am - 5pm Monday to Saturday, 12 - 5pm Sunday, Easter to end of October
Admission: Adults £2.25, OAPs £1.75, children 75p

3) Big L Factory Outlet
KINGSGATE RETAIL PARK, EAST KILBRIDE. G74 4UN
TEL: (013552) 41413
Open: 10am - 6pm Monday - Wednesday, 10am - 8pm Thursday and
Friday, 9am - 6pm Saturday, 10am - 5pm Sunday

4) Q Mark
BRAIDHOLM ROAD, GIFFNOCK, GLASGOW, SCOTLAND G46 6EB
TEL: 0141 633 3636
Open: 9am - 6pm Monday - Saturday, until 8pm on Thursday,
12 noon - 5pm Sunday

5) Pollok Country Park
2060 POLLOKSHAWS RD, GLASGOW
TEL: 0141 632 9299
Open: Park always. Admission: free

6) The Burrell Collection
POLLOK COUNTRY PARK, 2060 POLLOKSHAWS RD, GLASGOW G43
TEL: 0141 649 7151
Open: all year Monday - Saturday 10am -5pm, Sunday 11am - 5pm.
(closed 25th, 26th December and Ist, 2nd January)
Admission: Free

7) Pollok House
POLLOK COUNTRY PARK, 2060 POLLOKSHAWS RD, GLASGOW
Open: All year Mon - Sat 10am - 5pm, Sun 11am - 5pm.
Closed 25th-26th Dec & 1st - 2nd Jan
Admission: free

8) Antartex Village Visitor Centre
LOMOND INDUSTRIAL ESTATE, ALEXANDRIA, DUNBARTONSHIRE
G83 0TP
TEL: 01389 754263
Open: 10am - 6pm Mon - Sun.

TOUR 3
Alloa, Dollar, Lochleven and Perth

This tour starts at Alloa where at Tullibody Rd, Lornshill is the **Jaeger** factory shop. Here most of the merchandise is last season's stock and some seconds. There are now 14 Jaeger factory shops, some selling the whole range of Jaeger clothes, some just knitwear; yet others sell goods other than those with the Jaeger label. This shop has a good range of Viyella skirts, blouses and jackets as well as Jaeger skirts, £39-£59, dresses from £39, and jackets from £89-£129, all usually half price. There is also a wide selection of suits up to size 18.

From Alloa head north to Tillicoultry where you should then turn east up the A91 to Dollar. At Dollar, against the background of the beautiful Ochil Hills you will find 15th century **Castle Campbell** once the lowland base of the Argylls. There are wonderful views from the tower of the castle which can be reached by walking along the path through the stunning Glen Dollar.

From Dollar then carry on north east on the A91 for about ten miles when you turn off east on the B918 for Kinross and Lochleven. At Todd and Duncan near the M90 the **Lochleven Mill Shop** is situated. This shop sells Pringle sweaters and shirts at very competitive retail prices as well as its own cable cashmere at £70 which includes two-ply cashmere classic V-necks, crew-necks and roll collars; normal retail prices for these would normally be about £160. The shop also stocks lambswool sweaters for between £25-£60; Daks/Simpson skirts and jackets at competitive prices; Enrico cotton and angora mix skirts and tops from £12-£40 and other cheaper ranges.

From Kinross it is a quick journey up the M90 north to Junction 10 from where if you take the A93 four miles north (crossing the River Tay in the process) you will reach the **Palace of Scone**. Here was the old capital of Scotland in Pictish times and it was also from here that in 1296 Edward 1st of England took the Stone of Destiny upon which all Scottish Kings were crowned to become part of the Coronation Chair in Westminster Abbey. The exterior of the present building dates from the early 19th century but incorporates the 16th century building. The palace contains some marvellous displays of furniture, porcelain, clocks and ancient needlework and the grounds include gardens that can be brilliant at the right time of year.

One can't, of course, travel so near without visiting **Perth**, the

'Gateway to the Highlands' and a charming city. There is much to see there and amongst everything else it possesses, on the **Inveralmond Industrial Estate,** a factory shop and visitor centre that must be visited. On sale at the **Caithness Glass factory shop** can be found glass paperweights, fluted bud vases, fragrance bowls, limited edition paperweights, ornaments and glass at keen prices and occasional sales make for even better bargains.

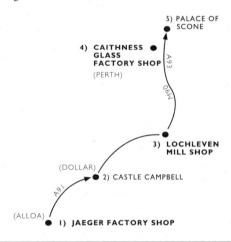

FACTFILE

1) Jaeger Factory Shop
TULLIBODY ROAD, LORNSHILL, ALLOA SK10 2EX
TEL: 01259 218985
Open: 10 am - 4pm Monday - Sunday

2) Castle Campbell
DOLLAR, CLACKMANNANSHIRE
TEL:0131 668 8800
Open: 9.30am - 4.30pm Monday - Saturday, 2pm - 4.30pm Sunday, closed all day Friday, October - March; 9.30am - 6.30pm Monday - Saturday, 2pm - 6pm Sunday, 1st April - 30th September.
Admission: £2 (children 75p, £1.25 OAPs)

3) Lochleven Mill Shop
TODD & DUNCAN, LOCHLEVEN MILLS, KINROSS (NEAR M90), TAYSIDE KY13 7DH
TEL: 01577 863521.
Open: 9am - 5.30pm Monday - Saturday

4) Palace of Scone
SCONE, TAYSIDE
TEL: 01738 552300
Open: 9.30am - 5pm everyday 5th April - 14th October,
Admission: £4.70 (children £2.60, OAPs £3.90, family ticket 2 adults and however many children £13.50)

5) Caithness Glass Factory & Visitor Centre
INVERALMOND INDUSTRIAL ESTATE, PERTH
TEL: 01738 637373.
Open Factory shop, 9am - 5pm Monday - Saturday all year, 10am - 5pm Sunday, April - October, 12 noon - 5pm Sunday November - March, to see glassmaking 9am - 4.30pm Monday - Friday all year.

TOUR 4
The Moray Firth, Fearn, Culloden Moor, Forres and Elgin

As you might expect, factory shops, (apart from those selling whisky!) are a little thin on the ground in this part of highland Scotland but there are definite compensations for the driving involved as you will pass through some truly breathtaking scenery.

The tour starts at Fearn, Rosshire, only a mile from the northern shore of the Moray Firth at the **Anta factory shop.** Here Anta make everything on site, using tartan check designs in traditional Scottish landscape colours and there are usually seconds and ends of lines available at discounted prices. There are jazzy check woollen rugs, carpets, luggage, fabric, salad bowls, throws, blankets and ceramics on sale at discounts of about 25%.

Also at Fearn there is the ruins of a **Premonstratensian Abbey** that moved here in 1298. At its height it was quite a substantial building with a nave, lady chapel, choir and two transepts completed in 1545.

After the reformation the Abbey became a parish church but in 1742 a dreadful accident occurred when on a Sunday the roof fell in, killing more than forty worshippers.

From Fearn take the A9 south following its picturesque route along the shores of the Firth of Cromarty to just south of Inverness. At the Culcabock roundabout take the B9006 east and it will bring you to **Culloden Moor** which was the scene of the last battle fought on the soil of the United Kingdom. It was here that on 16 April 1746 the Duke of Cumberland's army bloodily defeated the Jacobite clansmen of "Bonnie Prince" Charles Edward Stuart . In the ensuing rout the Duke's behaviour was such as to earn him the title of 'Butcher of Culloden'. A cairn built in 1881 marks the site of the battle and there is now also an information centre, museum, bookshop and restaurant at the site.

From Culloden driving east along the B9006 will bring you to the A96 which you should follow on to Forres. Here take the B9010 and it will take you to Elgin via the **Dallas Dhu distillery.** This is a fine old Victorian distillery which has been perfectly preserved and around which you are welcome to wander and partake of a dram.

Carrying on on the B9010 you will wind round east in a semi circle climbing above Dallas Forest and eventually coming down from the south west. At Elgin is your final shopping port of call is at **James Johnston of Elgin, Cashmere Visitors Centre,** New Mill. This is a factory shop with an on site visitors mill, where you can watch raw wool being made into luxurious cashmere – from the dyeing and blending through to the spinning, winding and weaving. Cashmere sweaters are sold here from £90 - £250 and there are regular bargain baskets.

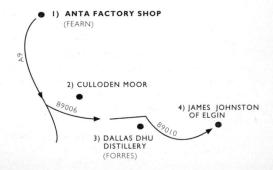

1) **ANTA FACTORY SHOP**
   (FEARN)

A9

2) CULLODEN MOOR

B9006

4) JAMES JOHNSTON
OF ELGIN

B9010

3) DALLAS DHU
   DISTILLERY
   (FORRES)

FACTFILE

1) Anta Factory Shop

FEARN, NR TAIN, ROSS-SHIRE IV20 1XW
TEL: 0186 283 2477
Open: 9am - 5pm Monday to Friday. 10am - 5pm Saturdays

2) Culloden Battlefield

CULLODEN MOOR, INVERNESS-SHIRE IV1 2ED
TEL: 01463 790607
Open: site all year. Visitor Centre: 9am - 6pm daily, April - October;
10am - 4pm daily 4th February, March and November - 30th
December (closed 25th, 26th December)
Admission: to Visitor Centre £2.60 (Concessions £1.70) pre-booked
party £2.10 each, childrens' school party £1 each, family ticket £6.90
(includes 2 adults and accompanying children).

3) Dallas Dhu Distiller

FORRES (1 MILE SOUTH OF FORRES ON A940)
TEL: 01309 676548
Open: all year 9.30am - 6.30pm Monday - Saturday, 2pm - 6.30pm
Sunday, April - Sept; 9.30am - 4.30pm Monday - Saturday, 2pm -
4.30pm Sunday, October - March (closed Thursday pm and Friday in
Winter and 25th and 26th December, 1st-3rd January)
Admission: £2.00 (children 75p, OAPs £1.25)

4) James Johnston of Elgin

CASHMERE VISITORS CENTRE, NEW MILL, ELGIN, GRAMPIAN
IV30 2AF
TEL: 01343 554000
Open: 9am - 5.30pm Monday - Saturday, 11am - 5 Sunday during
June, July, August, September